# The To-Do List Formula

The Guide to Create a To-Do List
that Improves Productivity and
Makes You Achieve Success

Dan Kristoph

Published by Krister Publishing

# TABLE OF CONTENTS

## PART 3: THE APPROACHES
## EXACT

## MEASURABLE

## AMBITIOUS

## ACHIEVABLE

## TIME-BOUND

## SUCCESS-ORIENTED

## ACCESSIBLE

# YOUR FREE GIFT

As a way to say thanks for reading one of my books, I would like to offer you my free e-book "**23 Good Habits in Life: The Simple Routine Practices that Can Make You More Positive, Happy, and Successful**". It is an 80-page e-book that talks about how good habits can make you a more positive, happy, and successful person. It also talks about how we can differentiate between good and bad habits. The main content, however, is the pick of 23 good habits that can be seriously impactful for your life. It will be a read that you might enjoy and it should a positive perspective for your personal development growth.

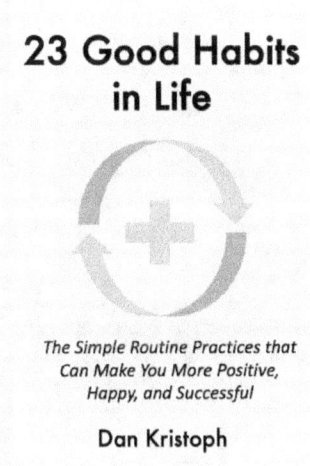

**23 Good Habits in Life**

*The Simple Routine Practices that Can Make You More Positive, Happy, and Successful*

**Dan Kristoph**

To grab your copy of this e-book, visit the link below and join my email list:
http://positivitystories.com/free-gift

In the following pages, we will talk about a simple yet impactful tool to organize your works, the to-do list. A to-do list can potentially be a powerful tool to significantly improve your productivity and direct your effort towards success. However, using it the wrong way and you might not get the positive impact that it can offer. It might even have a negative effect on the things that you want to work on.

Want to know more about how to create the to-do list that works? Let's dive into the content of the book starting the next page.

# FOREWORD: THE TO-DO LIST PARADOX

The usage of the to-do list has increasingly become a paradox that we simply don't want to happen.

According to the Cambridge Dictionary, a paradox is defined as **a situation or statement that seems impossible or is difficult to understand because it contains two opposite facts or characteristics**.

And according to the same dictionary, a to-do list is defined as **a list of tasks that you have to do, or things that you want to do**.

See the paradox of the to-do list yet?

Well, it turns out a to-do list can become the list of tasks that you **do not** want to do instead.

Do not believe me? Well, let's look at some statistics.

According to the data from iDoneThis, a check-in and progress report app, 41% of to-do items are never completed Moreover, only 15% of our completed tasks are the ones that originally reside in our to-do list. Looking at the data, it seems a to-do list has lost its meaning. Instead, it has become a tool that consists mostly of the things that we won't do.

Real shame for the tool said to be able to organize the works that we have and improve our productivity.

The question can come up because of this. Like, if we end up do not accomplish the tasks in the to-do list, then why bother utilizing it? When we decide to use something, we obviously want the benefits that come from its usage.

It seems not to be the case with the to-do list tool. And yet, there are interesting cases which illustrate that this tool has significant potential to help us with our works.

## The Importance of a Simple Yet Impactful Tool

Do you know Benjamin Franklin? He is famous for being one of the Founding Fathers of the United States. Interestingly, he is also one of the people who implement the to-do list in his daily routines.

During his years of work, he usually broke down his daily routine to the tasks that he wanted to do. He divided them into each window of the 24 hours a day available to him. He listed the things that he thought he should complete during the day so he can achieve his peak productivity.

It is something that fits a man who has done so much during his lifetime. The to-do list tool utilization is also suited with his famous quote which seems to become his life principle. That quote is "If you fail to plan, you are planning to fail."

Benjamin Franklin seems to somehow illustrate the potential of a to-do list. After all, he has achieved so much with his works. He is the person who invented numerous things with the lightning rod, odometer, and bifocals among them. He also started numerous civic organizations including the University of Pennsylvania. While at it, he wrote best-selling books and achieved some other important feats during his lifetime. Surely those things cannot be done by someone who has not been highly productive with his time.

The importance of a to-do list can be seen in a psychological trait of humans as well.

Have you ever heard of Zeigarnik Effect?

It is a psychological phenomenon. It says that our mind has a tendency to be fixated on the tasks that we haven't completed. On the other side, we tend to forget those which have been done. The simple example is when we work on some reports and we switch to create a presentation midway. When the report has not been finished yet, our mind can be distracted by the thought of that unfinished report.

It is something that interests Roy Baumeister and EJ Masicampo from Florida State University. To satisfy that interest, they run a research in which a group of people was asked to do a brainstorming task. The hitch is those people were given a simple warm-up task first before doing the brainstorming. During this research, they were asked to do the brainstorming before they finish that task.

It turned out that, as the Zeigarnik Effect suggests, those people did worse brainstorming session because of the prior task. Their minds are distracted by the thoughts of that unfinished task prior to the brainstorming.

What they do next in the research, however, signal one of the important functions of a to-do list for productivity.

Wanting to see the effect, Baumeister and Masicampo allowed some of the people to plan to finish the warm-up task. They did not finish the task. They just *planned* to finish it. The result of this treatment, though, is interesting. The people who could plan for the completion of the prior task can free their mind from the burden of it. As a result, they were able to be more optimal and productive during the brainstorming session.

What can be inferred from this in relation to the impact that we want from our to-do list tool? Well, it seems that the planning tasks with the to-do list can make our minds much more focused on current task.

The basic truth is our mind has a limited capacity. The fewer things that we should think about at once, the more optimal attention that we can give. Based on the research, by using a to-do list to plan our activities, we should be able to be more productive. That is because it helps to set our mind to one task only. By planning to do the other tasks besides our current task, our mind can be unbounded even before we finish them.

From the explanation given, it seems the to-do list has a considerable potential to become the tool that improves productivity significantly. If so, then how can we have low percentage to finish our tasks in it as illustrated by the previous data?

## The Wrong Approach
One of the most important things to maximize the benefits of using a tool is the way that we utilize it. The wrong approach can reduce the usefulness. It can even make the opposite impacts of the benefits that we hope to get from it.

This includes the to-do list as well. When we do not utilize the to-do list in the right way, it can even backfire on our daily productivity.

Need an illustration? Well, for a simple one, imagine you create a to-do list that is too long and the activity points are abstract. When you look at the to-do list to see the things you have to do, can that list demotivate you instead? You may think those tasks are impossible to do. As the motivation goes away, you may start to doubt why you have to do those activities in the first place. The urge of procrastination kicks in and you might neglect the things that you have to do as a result.

Maybe that is the thing that happens to you? I know that it has happened to me in the past before I improved how I do my to-do list significantly. The to-do list that you formulate to improve your productivity can have no to a little desired effect. It may even demotivate you when you need to do the works.

Surely, that is not our original intention when we start to utilize the tool.

### The Unproductive Rhythm

When you see something is recommended by people and you look at the benefits gotten, you will want to use that. The chance is you will continue to use the thing even though it seems to give you disadvantages instead.

I know that because that is what happens to me with the to-do list tool. In the past, I saw that the tool demotivated me from doing the tasks that I should do from the list. However, I then look at the productive people. They say that a to-do list is a tool that you should utilize for improved productivity. Therefore, I continue to use it even though it may even bring an unproductive effect on my work.

This creates an unproductive rhythm for the completion of my tasks. The to-do list makes you unmotivated to finish the works that you have listed in there. Nevertheless, you still formulate it because you think that it should help you with your works. That makes you unable to optimize your productivity as you are stuck with the habit of using the unproductive to-do list.

Well, it can be beneficial, of course. However, you have to learn the right approaches to optimize its utilization. As they say, doing things the same way over and over again will only yield the same result.

And, thus, this is why I wrote this book after I have improved the utilization of my to-do list considerably. I do that by learning from my experience utilizing the to-do list and also the best practices of using the tool. The book is written to share what I have known from the learnings.

By reading this book, you should catch the ideas how to get the intended benefits from the to-do list. I hope the content will be useful for you who also hope to maximize the impact of this tool too. Consequently, it should give positive impacts for the productivity of the works that you have to do.

**The Book Structure**

To achieve its objective as being stated above, I divide this book content generally to:

- **7 Mistakes that Make a To-Do List Highly Unproductive**
  As described before, a wrong approach in the utilization of a to-do list can make it gives less benefit to you. At worst, it can even make you become unproductive. In this part of the book, we will discuss the mistakes that people often make when they create a to-do list. After reading this part, you should be much more aware of them during your attempt to utilize the tool for yourself.

- **7 Characteristics of an Excellent To-Do List**
  As there are mistakes in to-do list implementation, there has got to be the right way to utilize the to-do list. The right to-do list comes with the characteristics that can eradicate those mistakes. The implementation of this kind of to-do list should be

able to give you its optimum productivity and success progress benefits. In this chapter, we will dig deeper into those characteristics to know what makes them the desirable traits of a to-do list. You should understand better about them for your optimum utilization of the tool after reading this part of the book.

- **The Approaches to Achieve Each Characteristic of a To-Do List that Works**
  After getting the knowledge of the desirable characteristics of the to-do list, we will learn about the approaches for those characteristics. Each characteristic of an excellent to-do list will be given three simple and practical approaches. This is meant to help you significantly in imbuing them to your own to-do list. Each approach will be given its own chapter explanation so you will know better about how it can be implemented. After reading this part, you should be able to practice those approaches to create a to-do list that works for you.

This book purpose is to give you ideas in creating a to-do list which can boost your productivity and success progress. To achieve its purpose, it has been given in a why-what-how structure as you may have noticed above. Hopefully, after finishing the book, you will be able to understand what can make a to-do list works for you. After that, you should be able to optimize the improvement benefits that you can get from your to-do list.

So, are you ready to learn more about the to-do list correct implementation? Let's get down to the mistakes that you can do when implementing it.

# 7 MISTAKES THAT MAKES A TO-DO LIST HIGHLY UNPRODUCTIVE

We all make mistakes sometimes on the things that we do. Especially if they are something that we do for just a short while.

When we utilize the to-do list first time, we might do something wrong that makes it unable to give its benefits. These wrong approaches are clearly the things that we should understand so we can fix them. In the long run, we can improve our to-do list implementation process so it can later give us the desired advantages. When we think about it, how can we do the right improvement if we don't understand things that we should improve? It is the basic principle of the improvement process for all the aspects of our life.

Yet, it is often not easy to know the wrong things that we have done related to our to-do list implementation. The ignorance of those mistakes makes them done for quite some time and they become a habit for us. When they have become habits, it can be harder to fix them. We might think it is a part of the to-do list implementation that makes it works for us.

For illustration, we may often create to-do list task points which are too general. Those task points may consist things such as finishing a project for our company or improving the sales of a product. These kinds of points can make us confused about what are the things that we have to do to finish them. They confuse us instead of giving us clarity regarding the completion of the things that we need to do. As a result, the to-do list that consists of things like these brings little improvement to the productivity of our work.

When it comes to acknowledging these mistakes, we may unable to do it. It is because the mistake is something that we have already done for a long time regarding our to-do list utilization. It became a problem as we continue doing something that gives us little or even opposite results of the intended benefits. We might just create the to-do list because we have got used to it. We don't consider the productivity benefits that we expect from the tool.

Therefore, it can be important to identify what are the mistakes that can be associated with the to-do list formulation. It is so that we know whether the mistakes are something that we do in our implementation as well. We can have more knowledge on their implication and fix them when we understand why they harm our to-do list usage. After all, it seems there is no use utilizing a to-do list if we make the mistakes in its implementation. Those mistakes that makes us cannot enjoy the benefits that we want.

To help you with identifying the mistakes, here are 7 main mistakes for the implementation of a to-do list. They might be the things that you still currently do so it is better to fix your to-do list formulation fast. Especially when you think they can bring bad impacts in your effort to organize your works optimally.

**Mistake #1: You Have Too Much to Do**
When creating a to-do list, it can be tempting to take the easiest path and just list all of our works. However, it might not be the best approach to implement. It can result in creating a to-do list which is abstract and just has too many things going on in it. The tasks listing of this nature will not bring the intended clarity that we can get from a to-do list.

There can be big things that we want to finish in our days. For example, we may want to finish fixing and cleaning our house or revise our work until our supervisor approved it. When we see these kinds of things listed, however, it might be demotivating because it is too general to follow. We may have no idea what we should do to finish the fixing and cleaning or complete the revision until approved. They are too fuzzy and can be drilled down better about the activities that we need to do to finish them.

The mistake of making too complicated points make us have to think hard so they can be regarded as done. This can potentially waste our time and lower our productivity as we try to figure out our to-do list meaning. The process can make us also doing things that are not meant for the best results of our work process. This all because we try to define how best we can finish the tasks in our to-do list. We can have too much to do as a result and that isn't good for our work's effectiveness and efficiency.

Besides having too much to do because of the tasks' ambiguity, the mistake can also be related to the tasks amount. Simply by having too many tasks listed can confuse us regarding what we need to do in a day. The implementation of this to-do list can make us bewildered of which are the tasks that really should be done today. Our time is limited so we might end up doing the tasks which might be not too important in comparison.

It can be simple to just list all the things that we want to finish on our to-do list. However, this mistake in the formulation can confuse ourselves when we try to do them. It might even lower our productivity as we don't know what are the right things to do in our working hours.

## Mistake #2: You Have to Do Things That Are Unclear

Besides too many things to do, we can also be confused by the unconcreted trait from the tasks that we list.

It is always easier to get the grip of something tangible rather than intangible and the quantitative rather than the qualitative. When we have tasks which are intangible and qualitatively measured, it can make us wonder whether they have already been completed. The results is we may prolong the time that is used to complete the task. It is because we do not know what is the defined finish line for it. Furthermore, we might also lose motivation because we don't understand how can we work for something that has no concrete objectives.

The examples are when we list something like improve our business or beautify the look of our garden. Because the points do not have clear goals in them, we may spend too much time working in them. We may even not work on them at all because we don't know what we can do to accomplish them.

The tasks that are too hard to define can be an important factor of the work which is ineffective and inefficient. When we don't know the things we desire from a process, then we won't know how the process should be shaped. This will lead to an unproductive effort. We try to create something that we do not know the exact requirements are. This is why a firm form of the outcomes that we want from our work is important. We will know what kind of work should we give and how much effort should we put into the process.

Moreover, when you want to measure the results to your expectation, you need to have something tangible you can compare. This is related to the next to-do lists also as it can use the measurement result for its formulation process. The missing quantifiable variables from your task's points will make it much harder to do this measurement and evaluation process. As a result, you may way too overestimate or underestimate the work that you do. This will affect the to-do list that you try to create for the next time.

## Mistake #3: You Have Too Easy Tasks

When you want to be productive, then you cannot just do your work with a so-so mentality. You need to push yourself so you can work optimally near your maximum capacity.

If you use a to-do list, then the way you list your tasks is crucial to determine your productivity. Sometimes, we want to take it easy by listing the tasks that can be done easily in a short time. This is not in line with the real benefits that we want to get from the tool.

We might get some satisfaction because we can finish all the tasks that we have already targeted so early. However, if we want to chase long-term success, then this can result in a much longer time for us to succeed.

Having too easy tasks listed is not ideal because it may become a strong reason for you to procrastinate. When we don't know what else to do, that is the time which we are prone to the urge of procrastination. When this is the case, that means our to-do list just becomes the tool that gives us validation to procrastinate. We might think, after all, the to-do list has been already done. We should use the remaining time to relax for the rest of the day. The to-do list that we create for productivity has just become the main reason to do the opposite. This is surely not a good habit to implement in our to-do list utilization.

Listing too easy tasks will also not push us to grow personally and professionally. One of the most important lessons that we can achieve can be had through the experiences that we got. The most valuable experiences usually come from the tough challenges that we face. When we only aim for the easy ones, that is when our self-improvement progress may stifle. This problem may also affect the future of our productivity. That is because the more you know about the way you should work, the more productive you are in getting results. As your growth is halted by the easy tasks' experiences, the chance to be more productive in future works isn't good.

It is easy to fall into the trap of making things too relaxing by placing not-so-difficult targets that we must accomplish. However, the highly productive people might choose the difficult ones rather than the easy ones. The criteria are the tasks are in line with their desired results. Moreover, they should be not too difficult that it may become another mistake in formulating the to-do list. The mistake of making it too difficult is what we will talk about next.

## Mistake #4: You Have Tasks that Are Unrealistic
It is all good if we want to challenge ourselves to complete all the tasks which we regard as most fruitful. This can bring the significant positive self-growth that we want from the experience of doing them. However, there is a case also of listing too many tasks to do in our to-do list. This mistake might even hinder the productivity benefits that we want to get from the tool. Unrealistically difficult tasks can become one of the main reasons for our low motivation to do them.

After all, an excellent to-do list should make us motivated to finish the tasks that are in it. Not the opposite.

When we formulate our to-do list, the general aim is to complete all the tasks which are listed in a day. This is because daily is mostly the cycle of a to-do list formulation. If we list many tasks which normally take time to complete, then rather than productive, it may make us lazy. It is because we may think there is no way we can do all of them in a day. When we already have a thought like that, it can make us even slower to do each of our works. That is because we have already lost motivation to complete all the tasks that our to-do list says we should do.

To make it clearer of the impact of this mistake, let's say that we do a to-do list daily. In it, we list that we should do a half-day meeting, finish 2 reports, and make a presentation. If we delve into those tasks, then we may know that it is almost impossible to finish all of them. The meeting takes half-day, maybe more if it is run late, and the report or the presentation should take a day. They may take even more if we want to produce the best results for them.

The insufficient hours can make us lose motivation to complete the to-do list. This is because we know that we simply cannot complete them. Even if we rush ourselves to complete all of them, then it most probably will not be good for the results. The results are bad because we cannot do our best for the details in each of them. It may even result in seriously bad outcomes which can hinder ourselves.

As a result of this mistake, the high productivity that we want when we list those tasks will not be had. It may even be hard for us to accomplish just part of the to-do list. The to-do list that we have already formulated may become redundant as we don't do the tasks that are listed.

## Mistake #5: You Have No Clear Deadline for the Tasks

This mistake should especially be had when we don't have a clear timeframe when all of the tasks should be completed. When we don't know the supposed deadlines of those tasks, we may tend to have a lower motivation to do them. This is because we may think we can do them anytime when we want. This may lead to lower self-discipline to finish our works, higher procrastination, and, eventually, lower productivity.

To illustrate this, let's imagine you are given a task to analyze some data. However, you don't have any deadline from your supervisor when does he/she expect that task to be completed. What will you do? Unless you assign a self-imposed deadline, it most possibly results in you don't try to complete it quickly. Because you don't know when you should finish the task, you may put it aside to complete the other tasks. You may even delay it when you have the free time in your working hours to finish the analysis. You give a low prioritization for the task. As a result, it will tend to be done in a much later time.

The importance of the deadline is also being stated in the result of researches. A research article done by Dan Ariely from Massachusetts Institute of Technology and Klaus Wertenbroch from INSEAD do this. It suggests that deadlines can help reduce the likelihood that you procrastinate. It is valid in both cases when they are self-imposed or when they are imposed by other people.

This seems a logical thing as deadlines, especially the tight ones, make us picking up the work pace. We cannot finish them any time we want as a result of this thinking. This tends to increase our productivity in doing our works.

Deadlines can make us more motivated to do tasks and their absence will make us more prone to abandon tasks. Therefore, it can disadvantage us when we don't give self-imposed deadlines for each task we have in our to-do list. Not having deadlines may make us take time too much in finishing tasks. This can result in us not completing the tasks we must do during the implementation period of our to-do list.

## Mistake #6: You Have a List that Goes Nowhere

Every one of us has long-term results that they want to achieve when they do something. For example, if we work as an employee in our company, then the long-term result might be promotion to senior positions. If we volunteer socially, the far future outcome that we aim might be a big social impact that can affect people. All of the works that we currently do can impact the likelihood of getting the best long-term results. The impact can be either positive or negative.

The short-term results may be more apparent and can be directly seen as the outcome that we get from our works. However, the long-term things should be given the attention as well if we want to realize them. If we want to achieve meaningful success, then logically what we do daily should also make us progress to that target.

This is where the mistake can be had on the to-do list that we formulate as well. We don't have the end game in mind when we list the tasks that we have to do. That can result in us much harder in achieving the long-term results that we want.

If you want to achieve a big success, then the tasks that you do should help you in getting there step-by-step. This cannot be helped by our to-do list if we just think about the short-term results. The things that we work on go nowhere in terms of the general direction that they lead us to. A part of that is being supported by the to-do list that we utilize to organize our works.

By implementing this mistake, that also means you aren't getting high productivity from your works. That is because some of them might be not the right things to do to get the results that matter. One of the important aspects of productivity is the meaning of the works that you do. The meaning should be highly relevant for you because that makes them the things you rightly focus on. When you tend to do works which don't affect you positively long-term, that means you have wasted opportunities. These are the opportunities that can be spent to do other more important things. Making the mistake of listing tasks that do not match with your desired long-term results can harm this aspect of productivity.

If you want your to-do list to bring success, you need to think of the success definition when you list tasks. You should formulate it so the contents are highly relevant to that definition.

**Mistake #7: You Have Difficult Access to the List**
To help you become productive through your to-do list, you shouldn't leave that list hard to access. This mistake can make you simply confuse yourself with the things you need to do according to your plan. There are times when you forget what you have formulated during your day. Not having the to-do list nearby to remind you can affect the productivity benefits that you can get from it.

After all, one of the list's main functions given is to remind you the things that you should accomplish, right? Having difficult access to the list during the day will neglect that function from the tool. You may run your day as if there is no to-do list to guide you.

The main reason for this mistake is simply because you put it in where you cannot just pick and see it. For example, you may just put it in a paper you left or in a note your laptop cannot access. Worse still, you may just think of those tasks in your head without putting them somewhere you can see. That can be the mistake that makes you forget easily the tasks and nullify the productivity boost from your to-do list. And it can happen because you just don't remember what is the plan you have made for your working hours.

The mistake of not making your to-do list accessible can also be related to the task points you have. Sometimes, the task nature is simply something crucial that you have to be reminded of. For example, it might be a meeting with someone important outside of the working hours. It may also be a little important detail that you should work for your report but it can be easily forgotten. When you make this mistake, it can make you forget those things you remembered when you formulate your to-do list. Those crucial things that you have noted to remind yourself might be the key to achieve the best results. You cannot remember them because you simply haven't got the easy access to see your to-do list.

\*\*\*\*\*\*\*\*\*\*\*\*\*\*\*\*\*\*\*\*\*\*\*\*\*\*\*\*\*\*\*\*\*\*\*\*\*\*\*\*\*\*\*\*\*\*\*\*\*\*\*

And thus, we should watch out those mistakes when we want to create a to-do list that works for us. Simply don't do things right in the important aspects of our to-do list can lower the advantages we got from it. It can even make us less productive when we use our to-do list.

Now, after we have identified the mistakes, now is the time we understand the characteristics that make the right to-do list. This is important so we know the things that we should aim for when we want to implement a to-do list. We will talk deeply about these characteristics in the following part of the book.

# 7 CHARACTERISTICS OF AN EXCELLENT TO-DO LIST

When you decide to use the to-do list tool, you must want its optimum benefits for productivity and success, right? Well, trying to formulate it based on some characteristics should help you significantly to get those benefits.

These characteristics of an excellent to-do list are given to answer each of the mistakes in the previous chapter. Think of them as antidotes so you can create an excellent to-do list that is free from those mistakes. This to-do list should help you in guiding your works so you can achieve the outcomes that you want.

To optimize the working hours that you have, you have to consider the right kind of tasks that you have to do. You also have to think what is the ideal time that you can allocate to each of them. The right kind of tasks means you listed the tasks that are meaningful for you. They also can be the effective & efficient ways to get you to the right quality of outcomes.

On the other hand, the ideal time should be the shortest time possible for you to produce your best works. When thinking about the right characteristics, there should be consideration about the to-do list that can list the right tasks. We should also think about the formulation of tasks grouping that can support high productivity during our days.

An excellent to-do list will guide you to make the most of your time. It is so you can be satisfied with the results that you have produced. Simply listing all the things that you have inside of your head won't work in creating a to-do list that works. It is better that you consider some relevant things related to your productivity when listing tasks. They can be your work commitment, the long-term results that you desire, or the tangible outcomes that you get. Making a to-do list that can balance all those factors should be your priority when you choose to utilize the tool.

Thinking about the characteristics that can solve to-do list mistakes and support in giving its utmost benefits can be challenging. Thus, to make it easier for you, you can see below the characteristics which should do just that for you. They are **exact, measurable, ambitious, achievable, time-bound, success-oriented, and accessible**. You can call them **EMAATSA** in acronym so you may have an easier time remembering them. These things should help you create the to-do list which gives you the most benefits in productivity and success achievement.

The following parts of this chapter will explain each of them in a bit. From the explanation, you have a better understanding of their application in the to-do list formulation.

### Exact

Utilizing the to-do list tool should make it much clearer for you about the tasks that you have to do. Therefore, it will great if the words there are straightforward but thorough enough. They will make you know exactly what you should do. Being exact in formulating the to-do list is a trait that is desired to create a to-do list that works.

This is the characteristic you can use to answer the mistake of having too much to do in your to-do list. Exact is about preciseness. It is how you should formulate the tasks listed so they can be simple and yet comprehensive. Applying the exact characteristic in your to-do list should make your tasks more organized. The characteristic should give you a solid understanding of what you should do in a much easier way.

Being comprehensive on something doesn't mean it should be complicated and having too much content. This is the thing that you should aim in your to-do list formulation process. A to-do list with too much going around can make you guess what you should do so you can complete it. It will not be good for the optimal productivity that you aim from the to-do list implementation.

Making your to-do list exact in here means the contents in the list are easy to understand. Ask yourself these questions. Will the tasks listed be easy to understand by other people who happen to read the list? Will they be able to know what they should do if they are being guided by the to-do list? Being able to answer them positively looking at your to-do list should indicate that the list already has the exact characteristic.

When having the desire to create a to-do list that works, it can be easy to fall into the trap of complicating things. You may list all the things that you want to be done with long explanation for each to make them clearer. However, that kind of list can make it fuzzy instead for you to complete all the points in it. The importance of making a to-do list which is sharp and straight to the point should be given its due. This is so you can accomplish your to-do list without having to think again what you should do. It should empower the productivity benefit as you don't waste any time thinking about what you should do from your list. Instead, you can directly go to execute them in the best way you can.

### Measurable
Being tangible and quantifiable is a good thing to pay attention to for all the targets that we create. This

characteristic should make it easy to evaluate our progress on and whether we have hit the targets or not. This is something that we want also for the tasks that we have in our to-do list. Being measurable like that is an aspect that should be the important trait of our list. Having a measurable characteristic should help us significantly in being objective related to what we execute from our to-do list.

Measurable means it is clear what we should do so the tasks in our to-do list can be considered as done. The things that can only be measured subjectively should be kept away. It is because it will depend on our interpretation of whether we have completed the tasks or not. We may choose the easy way by considering them done when we have worked on them for an insufficient time. On the opposite, we may think our works not done even if we have worked on them for a long time. This can be the case if we tend to look for every detail even the ones which are not too important. Those kinds of subjectivity should be avoided if we imbue the measurable aspect strongly to our to-do list. The characteristic will make us able to go through our tasks without being too stuck to one of them. The reason for being stuck can be that we don't know whether the things that we have accomplished are already enough. This is the thing that we want to prevent by being measurable in our to-do list.

The clear indicator of whether our tasks are done or not should help to boost our productivity. Our objective, after all, should be that we completed all the tasks in the to-do list that we have formulated. Doing so from an excellent to-do list should mean that we have been highly productive in the day. Being measurable on our points enables us to smoothly switch between tasks after each of them is done.

When we want to evaluate and fine-tune our work approach based on our list, having it measurable should also assure objectivity. We will know the rate of the completion and can reflect to make better planning for our next to-do lists. This can benefit us in progressively adding more productivity benefits from the next upgraded to-do lists. It should ensure that we optimize our to-do list implementation step-by-step.

Optimally adding the measurable aspect should mean we know what kinds of numbers that should be given to our tasks. This means you might benefit yourself with the knowledge of the numbers that should be given according to each task level. Having that knowledge will give you the ability to give objective numbers to your tasks which can be realistically completed.

## Ambitious

When you utilize the to-do list tool, that should mean you want to be more productive in your works. After all, you list your tasks because you want all of them to be done within a certain period. Moreover, they should be the activities you do so you can get you the results you desire. By adding the ambitious characteristic in your to-do list, you can aim for the most optimal result that you can get.

This characteristic is important if you want to achieve the most and gain the highest productivity benefits from your to-do list. Every day we have 24 hours to do our works and each person has got the same window of time. It is up to us to optimize it to get the best outcomes for our life. By being ambitious with our to-do list, we can make sure that we utilize each moment to something highly productive. Being ambitious means that we don't spare any effort to finish the tasks that can give us the desired outcomes. When we want to achieve our results as fast as possible, being ambitious with our to-do list is a must thing.

After all, one objective of using the to-do list is to organize works so you can accomplish many things, right? That is one of the productivity benefits that you should get from the tool. Being ambitious should help you get that benefit by making you much more ruthless with the time that you have. No to a little number of procrastination opportunities can be made available to us. This is because we try to accomplish most tasks that we have registered to our to-do list. An ambitious to-do list can inspire us to do so much more from the tasks that are listed in there.

Being ambitious should also help you in getting the best results from your work as fast as you can. As a result, it can also create much better progress for the success that you want to achieve. After all, the best results and success can only be gotten by the accumulation of our effort. Implement the ambitious characteristic in our to-do list and commit ourselves to get the tasks done. When you do that, you should be able to focus on the needed effort daily with a better and faster way. That is because you have the objective to finish the tasks from your to-do list. All of the tasks from an ambitious to-do list can give you much motivation to get the tasks done completely.

**Achievable**
Despite being ambitious with the tasks listed, we must also remember the limitation of hours that we have. Listing ambitious tasks while remembering the time needed to finish them is important to get the most from your list. Keeping your points achievable is essential so you don't feel too overwhelmed by the size of tasks you need to accomplish.

Having the tasks which can be done within our list's time frame will naturally support the desire to complete them. After all, we know from the formulation that they all can be done realistically. Believing the completion of all our tasks is realistic can keep us focused to do each of them faster and better. A to-do list which is ambitious but unrealistic can easily make us lose the motivation to complete all of our works. We may go through our days and we realize that we do not have enough time to do it. This is the main impact of making this to-do list mistake, which is listing unrealistic tasks, that we should avoid.

Making your to-do list achievable should also stimulate you to think about the most productive works that you should do. You don't have much space in your to-do list to register all the works that you can think of. Naturally, you should only pick the things which are most crucial to be worked on. Creating an achievable to-do list will make you much more selective in picking the right things to do for your days. Your productivity should be correctly directed by listing and doing only the things that you seriously should do. The time when you formulate your to-do list play a crucial role in making your work process more effective and efficient. That to-do list then will become the guidance that you need to make your works having the right kind of productivity.

The term "achievable" for the characteristic of your to-do list also relates to the resources that you have currently. The highest productivity should be gained by having a to-do list that can optimize resources to best support your work process. Focus on the achievable tasks based on the available resources when you formulate the to-do list. Doing that should enable you to list the tasks that you can finish without thinking about the resources you don't have. That unneeded thought may lower your productivity when you do the work. You will lose the motivation to finish the tasks that are difficult to do with the resources that you currently have.

**Time-Bound**

When you have some targets that you want to achieve, it is important that you set a time-bound characteristic for them. This is the thing that will make sure that you will be much more discipline in optimizing your time. Having this characteristic in your to-do list should give you more motivation to work. In turn, it will benefit you with more productivity to finish the works that you have listed in it.

The time-bound feature should be referred to regarding the period that you must spend and allocate consistently for all your tasks. As described earlier in the book, lack of time constraint can be a factor that lowers our productivity for a task. The reason is we tend to give low prioritization to those tasks because we feel we can finish them anytime. This is true particularly if you haven't grown a strong self-discipline to finish your works. Adding the time-bound characteristic in your to-do list should nullify the problem. It can also give the guidance that you need related to the prioritization of your tasks.

Having a time-bound characteristic should also give us more consideration regarding the evaluation and fine-tuning process of our work approach. One of the most referred indicators in determining our productivity is the time that we need to finish our work. Having the time-bound characteristic can be the way to see whether we are productive or not in executing our to-do list. In turn, we might improve the settings of the time limit for the tasks in our next to-do lists. The time limit shouldn't be too tight and enable us to do our best works. We can also improve our work approach so we can achieve the idealistic targets which we have set. Because of this, the time-bound characteristic can become the catalyst of the productivity benefit we get from our to-do list. This is especially related to the time needed to complete our works.

A to-do list with time-bound characteristics should give you an urgency sense as long as you are committed to complete it. When you execute your to-do list, think of the time constraint as something that you must meet. As a result of this, you should be able to enjoy the outcomes longer. Finishing your tasks faster might also give you the follow-up opportunities which you cannot get if you finish your tasks slowly.

## Success-Oriented

Surely, you want the results of your work to give you something meaningful. Regarding this, there is nothing better than the ones that will bring you much closer to the life success you want. Success is something that you have a strong desire to achieve and that objective can be helped by your to-do list. This can be the case as long as you apply the success-oriented characteristic during your to-do list formulation process.

A success-oriented characteristic should make you list the tasks that can progress you to the success that you want. This means that the results of your work should be directly or indirectly correlated with the terms of your success. Your work results should have much less meaning to you if they cannot contribute to the long-term success you desire, right? By having success-oriented characteristics, you could focus on the tasks that can be felt more meaningful when you have accomplished them.

Building the to-do lists that are success-oriented should help you to be more consistent in working towards your success. Success, after all, is something that should be constantly worked for. So, the to-do list should give you a considerable advantage related to the success that you want to achieve. Always looking at your desired success will make all your tasks to follow the same pattern and have the same purpose.

This kind of to-do list will help you to significantly give more attention and keep you moving forward towards your goals. That should help you in keeping on track with the short-term and long-term results that you intend to accomplish.

By considering success when formulating your task points, you can delay tasks that aren't suitable in terms of their results. They even probably should not be worked at all because they are not in line with your desired long-term results. The success-oriented characteristic will help you considerably in regards to listing the important tasks that you need to do. Your to-do list can help you to be more selective on the things that you should and shouldn't do.

Being success-oriented in your to-do list means you should balance between the short-term and the long-term results. This consideration can make you more productive related to the big accomplishments that you want in life. You should have this characteristic especially if you want a to-do list that can help you to achieve success in life.

## Accessible

One important function of a to-do list is to remind you about the important things that you need to work on. This is so you can optimize your day and make yourself highly productive. In this case, how you remember the important tasks that you have to do can affect your productivity. If you have a good memory of them, then you won't do the works which don't bring much impact to you. You won't spend time thinking about what you should do next after your current task is completed. For your to-do list to do this function optimally, it must have the accessible characteristic. Thus, you can easily take a look at it when you need some guidance of the works you have to do.

Think of the to-do list as a cheat sheet that you can read in case you forget what you should do. Having the chance to look at it again and again should also make the tasks plan stick themselves in your mind. As a result, the chance that you forget them even when you don't look at your list will be decreased. That can make you be more smoothly go through each of the tasks that you have.

It can be understandably hard to remember all the tasks listed as you go through the day. Especially if the tasks consist of small things that need to be remembered to work on. When you are in your working hours, your focus shift from one task or event to another. That will make you much more prone to forget things that are not related to the current task that you do. When a to-do list becomes accessible to you, it can guide you for the shift between tasks. You should have a firm knowledge of what you should do throughout as you are guided constantly by your list.

When you try to apply the accessible characteristic for your to-do list, that means you should have the list nearby. This is so you can see it as you need it. The to-do list may also have important details which you think crucial during the time when you should do your tasks. They can be important when you try to finish the tasks to get the best outcomes. By having your list easily accessible, that should improve the chance of it makes you remember those small but important things. That can affect your productivity positively as you don't miss any single thing that enables you produce the best results. You may even produce the outcomes faster as you already know the detailed things that you should do for the task.

\*\*\*\*\*\*\*\*\*\*\*\*\*\*\*\*\*\*\*\*\*\*\*\*\*\*\*\*\*\*\*\*\*\*\*\*\*\*\*\*\*\*\*\*\*\*\*\*

So, you have known deeper about the EMAATSA characteristics which can give you the optimum to-do list benefits. You may have the general picture in mind of the to-do list you will create the next time you formulate it. Try to incorporate these characteristics so you can prevent the mistakes which have been described in the previous chapter.

In the next chapters of the book, we are going to dig into the three approaches for each of the characteristics. Each approach can be implemented to make the EMAATSA characteristics stronger in your to-do list.

In brief, the approaches to strengthen each of the characteristics in your to-do list can be seen in the following table.

| Characteristics | Approaches |
|---|---|
| Exact | - Limit the scale<br>- Limit the topics<br>- Limit the sentences |
| Measurable | - Search for simple relevant data<br>- Benchmark the numbers<br>- Tie them to actions if needed |
| Ambitious | - Stretch your capability<br>- Remember the success arrival<br>- Compare the most successful ones |
| Achievable | - Look at the available time<br>- Think about the current resources<br>- Consider the most effective ways |
| Time-Bound | - Set the deadline<br>- Allocate specific time in the schedule<br>- See the long-term |
| Success-Oriented | - Have your grand goal in mind |

|  | - Prioritize the most important ones<br>- Reflect on the progress |
|---|---|
| Accessible | - Write it somewhere<br>- Make it easy to keep close<br>- Place reminders |

The three approaches for one characteristic should give you practical ideas about what to do when you implement the characteristic. You can read their explanation in the following chapters. Hopefully, they are able to make a significant positive difference to the way you formulate and use the to-do list.

So, without further ado, let's explore each of them so we can understand each of the approaches a bit better.

# EXACT APPROACH #1: LIMIT THE SCALE

If you want to implement the exact characteristic, one thing that can help you is limiting your task points' scale. This means your to-do list should consist of things that are not too abstract. They can also be easily translated to the activities that you should do.

When you do the scaling to your tasks, you need to also make sure that the tasks are not too small. Too small tasks mean you need to list many of them just to complete an ordinary work. The scale limitation consideration is important when you try to list the tasks that have an ideal scope in them. It is so they can be a reliable guide for you as you go through your day.

This approach is strongly related to the task breakdown process that you have to do when you formulate your to-do list. After all, any big works that you have should be able to be broken up into more detailed tasks. Those tasks can also be divided again and again if you want them to.

For an illustration on this, when you have a project to work, then this kind of work can be broken down. The smaller works can be:

- Discuss with your colleagues about the project
- Do the data analysis that is needed for the optimal implementation of the project
- Make the presentation related to the project
- Make the progress report
- Evaluate the project implementation
- Some other works that you have to do to finish the project completely

When you look at it deeper, that discussion with colleagues can also be broken down again to things such as:

- Planning the meeting
- Creating the discussion points
- Inviting the colleagues and other people who might be important
- Other activities that can make the discussion produce the best outcomes.

There can be many scaling that you can do with your tasks as you can see a bit in the illustration. When you try to determine the good scale of those tasks, then there are several things to think about. The ideal scaling process should make each task not too big to overwhelm you and not too small to be insignificant. Think about the scale of work that can make you feel the most motivated to do them. For the purpose of setting guidance, you may want consider the duration to finish the task in your schedule. Probably the minimum of 30 minutes and the maximum of one hour for each task should do. This can be a limitation standard when you think about the size of tasks that you put into your to-do list. This consideration should make the task not too long to complete that you cannot shift your mind to other important tasks. It should also be not too short to make your to-do list bulge up too much. This approach should also help you determine how many task points ideally that you have in your to-do list.

Another good indicator for your task points can be seen also from the clarity of them. When you read the tasks in your list, you should know what are the things you should do to complete them. Are they clear enough to guide you when you go through the day which has been organized by your to-do list? Read the points again after you finish listing down your tasks. If you find yourself confused with the scale, then it is better to adjust so it can be clearer for you. When they are too general in language, then usually the good idea is to scale them down to be more precise. Be considerate with the scale to make your to-do list much easier to be implemented.

One thing that you might pay attention to when you scale tasks is the opportunity you have with other big tasks. You don't want to make your to-do list full with breakdown of one big task without considering the cruciality of others. Actually, this can be one of the advantages by having a great task breakdown. If you can utilize it well, there can be some space for smaller tasks from more than one big tasks. Try to consider all of the tasks that you have when creating the task breakdown for the scaling. This is so you have a to-do list that works the best for the results that you want to accomplish.

# EXACT APPROACH #2: LIMIT THE TOPICS

Another thing that you can do to make your to-do list has the exact characteristic is to limit the topics. As has been explained before in the topic of limiting the scale, there is an advantage of scaling your tasks correctly. You can put in those ideal scale tasks that you deem should be done in that day from different big tasks. However, if it isn't necessary, then you might want to limit the topic of your to-do list as few as possible. This should help to improve your focus at work while also boosting your productivity as a result.

It is simply not recommended to have too many tasks-switching if you don't need to. According to the American Psychology Association, we can lose 40 percent of our productivity by continually switch task. That is quite the cost that you have to pay if you concern about your productivity at work. Thus, we should do our best to limit this task-switching process in our daily works.

You may also have the feeling that you will lose productivity if you do this task-switching too much. For example, there might be past instances when you do the task from this one topic of work. Then, you need to work on a completely different topic after it is done. What do you feel about your focus? Don't you feel that your mind is harder to get ignited to focus on that new task? When you have a to-do list that has exact characteristics, then you should be able to minimize this productivity problem. By limiting the topics of our to-do list, we can improve our focus on the tasks at hand.

To help limiting your to-do list topics, you can think about the smaller tasks from one big task as a block. When you don't have smaller tasks from other big tasks that are crucial to be done fast, then this is great. You should put one kind of block into one day of your to-do list. That should help your focus to be pushed high all the time from when you start to do your work. If done in a block, then your previous task's results might even help you in getting it done in subsequent tasks. That can be the case if you are disciplined in keeping the smaller tasks from one big task in one sequence. After all, they are still correlated strongly in terms of their topics.

When limiting your list's topics, you might also want to consider doing topics linking when you need to combine topics. For example, you might see the linkage in these two topics:

- Improving the sales performance of product A
- Improving the marketing strategy of the whole business

Marketing and sales can support each other in terms of their function. Therefore, their tasks breakdown can be put in one day by considering their close relationship and the cruciality of them.

By having related topics to be worked at one go instead of distinct topics, it should help you with your focus. The stronger relationship that the tasks have, the easier should it be for you to do the task-switching. This can affect your productivity positively in a considerable way.

When we talk about the topic's limitation in our to-do list, we can also discuss the topic in each task point. In this case, we want it to be focused on one topic only per item. This treatment can help to make the task points clearer to us. It will also help the task to be not redundant with one another.

Here is an example of the thing that we want to avoid by this. See these two task points:

- Create the outcomes of the data analysis to create reports
- Make the recommendation in the progress reports

These two might bump to each other because more than one topic that can be associated with each of them. The reports that can be more than one and the nature of the tasks that can overlap each other. The bumps that we have among the tasks might make us confuse on what should we do in each task. That can be not good for the clarity that we expect from each of the tasks in our to-do list.

# EXACT APPROACH #3: LIMIT THE SENTENCES

After we explore how to limit the scale and topic, now we discuss how to limit sentences in the to-do list. This approach should help keeping the tasks concise by considering the length that the sentences have on our to-do list. As a result of this exact approach, we should understand better our tasks when we need to refer to our list.

It is simply easier and more motivating to understand the short sentences rather than the long ones. The long sentences can impact the readability of the points in our to-do list. They make it more complicated for us to comprehend the things that we have listed in the list. As we need to see it occasionally, the hard-to-read sentences can confuse and even demotivate us in completing tasks. We might become alienated about the things that we should do after we look at our to-do list.

The simple truth is our brain always prefers to have something simple and not complicated. Therefore, it is to our advantage that we try to make our sentences much more precise in our to-do list. We will make sure our brain is more motivated to go through the tasks and do the things that are listed. After all, when we can make things simple, why do we have to make it complicated to understand? Doing so will only make a loss for ourselves as we are the ones who utilize the things that we write.

To start limiting sentences, we should know the limitation requirement of our to-do list to make it much simpler to understand. How far should we limit the sentences in its task points? We might want to refer to the words counts for setting the limitation in our to-do list formulation. According to Rudolf Flesch and his readability formula, 8 or fewer words in a sentence should be very easy to understand. The limit is 14 words which can still be described as easy-to-read while 21 words is the limit for normal difficulty. Looking at this guide, then we should target these word counts for the tasks' sentences that we formulate in our to-do list. Try to describe the tasks clearly with 21 as the maximum number of words in them. That should help in making our task points much simpler and easier to understand

If you think that your tasks need more words, then it can be good to break them down into more points. Or probably, try to make them more summarized. For example, you may have written a task that says "Clean the house completely by making sure that the rooms are well organized and all the things are being put into their place". You might want to break down the sentence or summarize it so you can make your sentences easier to understand. For the breaking down process, you can make the long sentence to points like these:

- Mop the floors
- Throw away unneeded items
- Put goods into their place

Doing so should make task points are more precise. You can also summarize it to "organize stuff in the rooms". If you think that is enough to get results you want, then go for it.

From the example above, you should also see the illustration of the motivation that shorter task points can give you, right? You can see here the impact difference between the long and short sentences for your task points. The shorter ones will help you to be more driven to do them when you read them. Therefore, it can be crucial to break down or summarize the long sentences that you have in your list. It can help you to get additional productivity improvement that you need from the to-do list tool.

Limiting the sentences also help you to concise the topics of your tasks into one point. As has been told in limiting topics, that should help you make the tasks not redundant with the other tasks. Knowing that you have limited words you can use should "force" to reduce the things described by the task. Think of one point that you want to associate with your task then write the task sentence on your to-do list.

# MEASURABLE APPROACH #1: SEARCH FOR SIMPLE RELEVANT DATA

The important thing about adding the measurable characteristic in your to-do list is to give something tangible and quantifiable to tasks. This is so you know when to say that the tasks are done. This measurable aspect can also be used to evaluate your productivity whether it is according to plan or not.

It can be easy to add the numbers that make your tasks measurable if you have experience in doing the tasks. You may already know what can be called as the ideal results of them by looking from that experience. However, if you don't have the experience before, then you might want to look for some information. This can also be important when you want some comparisons to the numbers that you think as good for your tasks. One of the sources from which you can have the information is the relevant data for the results of the tasks. This data can be found in online or offline media as long as it is reliable.

The data that can help you to define the expected results of your tasks may not give you direct answers. However, you can probe them to get expectation numbers that should be close to the things that you want to do. For example, you may not find the numeric data of a report that can be assessed as excellent by your supervisor. However, you may find the numeric data that is related to the aspects that you should have in an excellent report. By keeping open thinking to the data related to your tasks, you could find those that can predict the best outcomes. This can be done even if you don't find a direct data related to the results that you want.

# MEASURABLE APPROACH #2: BENCHMARK THE NUMBERS

When you want to find the ideal results for your tasks, you can do worse than doing the benchmarking process. Numbers benchmarking can be the source of important insight to create an excellent measurable characteristic to your to-do list. This might also be the comparison that you need with your experience of the results when doing the tasks. After all, you will know how you perform compared to the best and the average ones from the benchmarking process. This ensures that you are not blinded with the subjective perspective for your results.

For an illustration of the subjectiveness, you might think what you do in the past is already enough for your task. Therefore, you set that past outcome from your experience as the thing that you target with your current to-do list. However, after you benchmark with people doing a similar task, you might find that you lag behind from the average performance. As a result, you have the motivation to increase the expected results numbers to equal or even exceed that average performance. Not doing the benchmarking will make you keep doing the low performance for the task. You might never know that it is not a good result to have. That is simply not healthy for the best results that you expect from the task you add in your to-do list.

When you target to improve productivity from your to-do list, the impact from the benchmarking process should also be great. This is true especially if you benchmark from the best practices which yield the best results for your kind of task. After all, one of the productivity traits is you should produce the best results with the time that you have, right?

By giving the numbers targets from benchmarking the best, you should be more motivated in putting in the best effort possible. They have been done before by other people so you should know that the results are possible. This should also logically help you to progress faster to the success that you want related to your tasks.

By doing the benchmarking, you may also get to know the process to produce those excellent numbers for the results. The way to do things in the best way can be learned and that should help you get excellent outcomes too. You may also want to add to your to-do list the task points related to the approaches that you learn. They are among the best way to do your tasks at the moment which might apply too for your situation.

What are the sources of benchmarking that you can look at? There are many. One of them is the online media and you should be able to find it fast using the search engine. Look for the best results which people have produced by doing the same task that you want to do. There are often number data of the results which you can compare with the task results that you may have targeted. Consider the numbers that you have benchmarked and add the consideration results to the tasks in your to-do list.

There might also be some experts in the area of your tasks. When doing the benchmarking, consider taking a look at the results that they have produced by doing similar task. That can give you the inspiration that you can do the same. You might even be tempted to implement a similar approach with them to do your work. You can target them so you are more driven to find a way to produce the same kind of results. If you have a related mentor, this is a great time to know more about the results that you can expect. Discuss with the mentor about what is the result you can expect from the task. Discuss also what can you do to achieve it like that.

You can also take a look at the results that have been produced by the people around you when you benchmark. The result of this might be more relevant to you as they should have a similar condition when they do it. If you know the people who produce good results, then try to discuss to see their perspective of the results. You might also want to dig deeper into the way they use to do the task. This can be further material for you to refine your way of doing your task to a better one.

# MEASURABLE APPROACH #3: TIE THEM TO ACTIONS IF NEEDED

If the task listed in your to-do list produce intangible results, then it can be hard to give numbered targets. This condition can confuse us regarding the measurable characteristic that we should add for your to-do list.

For illustration, you may have tasks like spending some time with your family or doing some jogging on your list. They can be the kinds of activities that might be hard to say when they are done based on the results. After all, you cannot measure the results directly during the time when you do the tasks.

There is a solution to this, though. For these kinds of task points in your to-do list, you can also add the measurable characteristic. This can be done by tying the tangible aspects of the tasks to the actions that you take when working. Giving some numbers that can be measured regarding the process of the actions will help you to do that.

Adding the numbers should help to give a sense of closure to the tasks that you do. By implementing the approach, you will know when you have finished them even though you cannot measure the results directly. Moreover, you can also measure your productivity simply by comparing the numbers you do with the ideal time for the activity. You can measure by asking the question: have you been able to do the actions numbers according to the time given? That can be some sort of evaluation basis that you can use when you try to reflect on your to-do list. That can be done even if you don't have the result numbers to do that.

To add this tangible aspect to your actions, you should see what are the possible numbers that you can add. It can be how many times you do the action or the duration in which you act on them. The one that you add should be relevant to the tasks that you have in your to-do list. Different cases may require different kinds of numbers attached to them. It can also be the case of picking the best number type if there is more than one that seem compatible. Add the one that you think can give you a higher productivity boost in your to-do list.

Besides the actions-related quantity, it will be nice if you can add some sort of standardization to your tasks. The standard can make it clearer for you on how you should do your task. You will be more motivated to maintain quality in your actions instead of just getting them done. This can be important when you don't have the results that you can measure the quality of your tasks against.

For the quantity and standard you give, you should obviously make them in line with the expected results from the actions. The quantity and standard should logically give you improvement to the result even if the result is something intangible. Think about what things you can do related to those aspects so you can make your actions produce the best results. After you have considered them, add the specification of them to the tasks that you add in the to-do list. That is if it is possible and seems to help you in boosting productivity.

For an illustration of this approach, let's take a look at the previous tasks that produce intangible results. If you want to add measurable characteristics to those tasks, then you might list them like this in your to-do list:
- Spend time with your family for 1 hour a day
- Do the jogging with the distance of 1 kilometer

The numbers added can give you the idea of how you can consider them as completed. You might also want to add things like no smartphone during your family time to give the standard that you need. This standard should increase the quality time that you spend on your family as a result.

It can be sometimes hard when you want to add some tangible aspects to the tasks in your to-do list. There are two things that you can do: add it to the expected results or to the actions directly. Adding it to your actions is a good thing to do also. It still can give the benefits that you want to get from the measurable characteristic of your to-do list.

# AMBITIOUS APPROACH #1: STRETCH YOUR CAPABILITY

The ambitious characteristic is about finding the ways to produce as many results as possible within the available time. Using the to-do list, that can be done by adding the detail which can bring the best productivity out of you. When you formulate the list, you should stretch your capability to optimize the opportunities that you have for doing your work.

When it comes to stretching your capability, mostly it concerns itself with the time that you allocate for the tasks' completion. The list can often become the expectations that you have for yourself regarding the tasks you can complete. Have you already expected the best effort from you considering the time that you have? The answer to this is important when you consider that your expectation often becomes your reality.

Ever heard of the Parkinson Law? It is a popular law about the human approach to work. It says that "work expands so as to fill the time available".

That doesn't mean that if you allocate thirty seconds to your two-hours work, then it can be completed well accordingly. This law is a result of an observation process of the bureaucracy in an organization, after all. It is related to the situation when you prolong the expectation of your work completion way more than it should be. The law says in this condition, most of the time, your work will be eventually completed in that prolonged duration. Even sometimes more. It seems as humans, we tend to spend time as much as we can to finish work. If we have the chance, then we may try to delay our work completion as long as it is permitted.

That is what expectations can do to your work process. Now, what is the implication of this to the to-do list that we formulate? Well, think of the to-do list as the expectation that we have for the completion of our tasks. Let's say you are too soft in the expectation by listing a small number of easy tasks to complete every day. According to the law, those tasks will fill up the time that they are given. It can be because you slack off during the work process or you choose to procrastinate greatly in between. After all, you can do that because you have set a low expectation of your productivity. It is bad. The to-do list has become an excuse for you to be unproductive.

Of course, doing this will not give you the benefits that you seek from utilizing the tool in the first place (except if the justification of procrastination is your objective). When you allocate too much time for your work, the opportunity to utilize that time cannot be gotten back. You should be able to finish so much work but you choose to finish only a small part of it. That is a sad part.

So, it seems obvious what you should do to stretch your capability, right? To optimize your productivity to the highest, you should set ideal self-imposed deadlines for your tasks. Think about the minimum time you need to complete each of the tasks and formulate your to-do list with that assumption. This should make you be able to fill up the to-do list with more tasks than usual.

As you implement your to-do list, you can test whether the assumption of that minimum time is true for each task. You might hit it spot on or give yourself more time than you should have. If the second assumption is right, then you should be stricter with yourself the next time you formulate your to-do list. That can help you to be more disciplined and productive in utilizing the time that you have for work. Your to-do list will become progressively beneficial as you keep on fine-tuning it to implement the ambitious characteristic further.

It is important to treat the self-imposed deadlines as the deadlines from external sources. Not that you should tell people to give you strict deadlines because that potentially will stress you out. You should simply make your self-imposed deadlines as if they are given by other people. To do that, do not slack off in the work process thinking that the to-do list has pushed yourself too hard. Try your hardest to complete the to-do list based on the strict deadlines so you can benefit in terms of productivity. If there is no firm commitment to finish the to-do list, then that can be a further reason for procrastination. It will diminish the effect of ambitious characteristics that you have wanted to place in your to-do list.

# AMBITIOUS APPROACH #2: REMEMBER THE SUCCESS ARRIVAL

When it comes to success in life, you want it to happen as soon as possible, right? If it is a matter of when not if, then the faster the better. After all, you can enjoy success for a much longer time if you happen to accomplish it faster. Success is the ideal condition that we want in life, whatever our definition to it is. So, it should be a great thing for you to be able to quicken its arrival.

If that is the case, then you should want to work as much as possible in a shorter period of time. If you are serious about wanting to achieve success, then it is hard to find another way. As long as you direct your work to the success that you want, then it will surely take you there gradually. When you do more work faster, then logically you should get the benefits from the work results faster too. You should also be able to improve your approach to work as you accumulate experience. That experience can be gained faster too if you can finish up more works in a shorter time.

This is a simple yet effective principle of some ambitious people. It is why they choose to work hard for a long time. They know that success is something that you should work for. The productivity of your work should be in line with when the success will come. The higher productivity you utilize in work, the faster your success should come. The opposite is also true.

When you utilize the to-do list to organize your work, then your desire for success should be reflected in its content. Do you want to achieve success fast? Then, you should fill up your to-do list with as much relevant work as possible. Do not waste the space that you can use to accomplish more work. Doing that should ensure that you have done all you can to progress faster to the success that you desire. Applying the ambitious characteristic to your to-do list is important for your success arrival as it seems.

To be ambitious with your to-do list, try to set it to your mind about this principle of success arrival. When you have done tasks related to it, then imagine you get one step closer to the success that you want. No one may know how many steps you have to take. Different people may have different steps to take. It can be affected, after all, by the unique circumstances of each person. However, taking it step-by-step simply will make the success to be closer and closer to you. As you try to be ambitious, you can set as many tasks as possible on your to-do list. That should speed up the step-by-step approach for you.

Think about your success as a destination that you want to go to. Next, think of the works that you do as the effort that you need to put in to get there. If you don't complete your tasks, then you will stay where you are. Now, what do you think you need to do to get to your destination? In the shortest time possible? You need to complete the tasks that you have as fast as you can, of course.

Let the formulation of your to-do list helps to organize that for you. When you still have the space to do your work, do not let it go away. Take the opportunity to complete more tasks so you can finish as much as you can. When there are some tasks that are still long overdue, push yourself to start completing it. You may not know that you will not have much chance to finish it in the future. Utilize the time that you can to be productive. The time that has gone cannot be gotten back, after all.

To make the success arrival faster, you may also need to keep developing your knowledge and skills for the better. If you have got the time, then it will be good to allocate it for your learning activities. Know what are the lessons that you need to have to be more productive in your work. There can be many sources where you can learn it, offline and online. Utilize them so you can be a better person who can work effectively and efficiently for your tasks. The time that you have for work should be used more productively. The results of your learning activities should benefit your work to produce more and better results also.

# AMBITIOUS APPROACH #3: COMPARE TO THE MOST SUCCESSFUL ONES

Do you need more motivation to be ambitious? Well, just look at the most successful people in your work area. That can give you the motivation that you need. As long as you believe in your capability and think you can be like them, it can serve as a boost. This boost will give you the thoughts to keep working and utilize your time optimally. This is so you can have the chance to be as successful as the most successful people. Even exceed them. Your to-do list may serve as the way to get the most productivity for your work.

It can be easy to be impressed by the success that people have. But, if the successful people you know start from the bottom, then do you read their success stories too? Those can be a strong source of inspiration when you learn about their stories. When you know they work hard to get where they are now, you will want to do the same. They struggle and yet they succeed in the end. Some of them may have had the condition worse than us during the journey to success. Yet, they consistently put in the highest effort to be at the top of their area. Now, they enjoy the fruits of their labor. One of the important factors is because they have been ambitious with their work.

When you want to utilize your to-do list to get optimum results, you need to have an ambitious characteristic as well. Fill the tasks in it so you can work hard as those most successful people when they work for their success. Think about it as the way you travel on the road to success as them. There is no success that can be gotten without putting in the effort, after all. If you happen to organize your work with a to-do list, then you need to plan your works accordingly.

75

Make your to-do list a way to set up the completion of tasks that utilize the most productivity for you.

Your objective, after all, is the position where the most successful people are. It is hard for most people to get there. Therefore, you should work to bridge the gap that you have currently with them. If that gap is huge, then that means you need to work as hard as you can to close it fast. The to-do list that you formulate will determine that. The question is: are you willing to do that? Being highly productive means allocating as many works as possible in your to-do list. That is the requirement if you want to succeed as the most successful people.

If successful people that you look at is in the same work area as you, then it can be better. If not, it might benefit you to find other people for that. Look at the things that they work on to achieve success. Some of those works can be needed too by you but you haven't put them in your to-do list. Reflect on the tasks that are in your to-do list by comparing them to the work done by the successful people. It can be an important lesson for you. You may find that you lack things in your to-do list. That lack probably can be compensated by mirroring the approach to work from the most successful people. The tasks that they accomplish can also serve as the ideas of your work in the to-do list. You might benefit by getting the knowledge of them more in terms of their work process.

To learn from successful people, you can also learn about their daily routine. How do they set up themselves every day? What is their typical schedule for work? You may learn a thing or two about how to set up your to-do list to be ambitious that way. Usually, the most successful people have some regularity that they follow so they can work productively. Learning from them can build up this approach too when you formulate your to-do list. You should be inspired to put on most tasks that can be worked in the period of your to-do list. That should serve as the ambitious characteristic implementation in your list.

The most successful people are usually those who work the hardest. Try to formulate your to-do list according to your motivation to be like them. There must be some successful people that serve as inspiration for you. Try to see how they work might be important to deliver the to-do list that gives you the most benefit.

# ACHIEVABLE APPROACH #1: LOOK AT THE AVAILABLE TIME

After discussing how to be ambitious with your to-do list, now we discuss how that ambition can be achievable.

There are some constraints that you want to consider when you allocate tasks in the to-do list. When it is true you want to put in as many tasks as possible to your list, you have your limit. That limit is mostly related to the time that you have available. After all, no one gets more than 24 hours a day. Thus, no one can work on their daily tasks more than that number of hours that they have. Because of that, there is a certain task quota that can be added to your to-do list. You shouldn't exceed this quota too far if you want your to-do list to be strongly motivating.

You would want your to-do list to make you driven to finish all the tasks that you have. However, having too many tasks to complete in a period can be off-putting.

Maybe you had experienced a period when you just get overwhelmed by your workload in the past. What is the feeling like? Instead of getting driven to get them done, you may become lazier to work. That is because of the belief that you cannot get them done in time. Instead of being pushed to be productive, the effect might be the opposite. If you still work on them, then you might just do it normally because you know you cannot finish. This situation won't give the productivity benefit that you want for you.

So, this is why achievable characteristic is also important to have in your to-do list. One important approach to help you get that characteristic is to understand the available time that you have for your tasks.

79

Most of us have 8 hours to work every day (probably more if you choose to add them). Different days may have different times available for you. For example, maybe one day you have a vacation with your family so you don't work at all. On the other day, you may need to stay at the office longer to prepare something for your work. During this limited and fluctuating amount of time, what can we accomplish? Think about it in mind as you make your to-do list. That should help you in determining the tasks which can be realistically put in there. Not too many to make it demotivating but not too few to make your time not optimized.

As you learned the ideal time you need to do each task previously, that knowledge should help you. Identify the time that you have with the duration that you need for each of the tasks. As the ideal time is the minimum duration to complete a task, you should be able to list more tasks. Allocate smartly in your to-do list and do not exceed the available time too much if you can. You may need to think also about the miscellaneous activities such as transportation, lunch break, etc. Those things may reduce the available time that you have significantly if added up. This thinking can make it clearer for you about the available time that you have for all of your tasks.

When looking at the available time that you have for tasks, you can also think about the possible additional time. If needed, then there can be some slot in your schedule which you can use to work. For example, the time that you have for lunch can be used to work while eating if you must. If what you work on is something urgent or you want to finish it fast, then you want to utilize them. Potentially, you can finish more by allocating tasks to be done at that time. However, you might not want to do this too much as you should allocate some time to rest to avoid burnout.

Having considered the expected available time previously, there might be a time when you need to face some sudden works. That can happen as you go through your days and it may disturb the tasks that you have planned to do. If that is the case, then try to take a quick look at your to-do list to reorganize. Consider the time that you need to give to finish the sudden works. How does that affect your available time? Look at the tasks that you have and try to see what are the things that can still be delayed today. You may need to cross off some tasks so you can work on all that are left. Another option might be to add some additional time to work that day. Consider the situation that you have to decide which best option you should choose.

# ACHIEVABLE APPROACH #2: THINK ABOUT THE CURRENT RESOURCES

After considering the time you have to make your to-do list achievable, the next consideration is the resources that you have. The current resources that can support your work might be limited and they should be considered. Of course, they can be expanded in the future so you can work with more flexibility. However, there are constraints to your work that can be caused by your current condition. That must be watched out when adding some tasks on your to-do list.

The limitation of current resources can cause some tasks to be harder to do so that can add to your thinking. For example, you may have limited networking capability and that can affect your way to do business development related tasks. Or probably, you have limited financial capability and that can change the best option to spend some family time. Considering the limitation of resources that you have, it may simply be better to act on one task than another.

The tasks that you want to add in your to-do list can have different sets of resources associated with them. It might need to utilize the facilities that you have, human resources, money, and other kinds of limited resources. You must look at the kind of tasks and what are the options available to you looking at the current resources. Can you do the thing that you want to add to your to-do list or not? You may also want to look at the allocation of the resources because they might be needed by your other tasks. You may need to utilize them more in the other tasks than the ones you add in the current to-do list. You should try to optimize their use so they can give you the best results based on your condition.

For example, you may have limited money for your vacation and you want to consider the preparation tasks for it. What are the best options? You may want to go to several tourist places, book hotels, or decide the transportation options. Each of their use to your financial resources will affect the other preparation tasks and thus, you need to choose wisely. It is so you can have the best outcome from the selected preparation tasks added to your to-do list.

To determine the best options, you might need to allocate a special task in your to-do list to think about it. This can be especially needed when you need to allocate for some important tasks. If it is the potential outcomes are important for you, then you cannot choose your options deliberately. Make sure you have enough time to think and decide your options. List all the limited resources that you have and the task options that you can do. From there, you can prioritize the task based on their potential outcomes. Based on the prioritization, you should be able to allocate your resources to the best task options that you have. From there, you can add those selected tasks to your to-do list. Doing it this way should help to give you potentially best outcomes from the limited resources for your tasks.

When doing the exercise, you should put the thought process somewhere. After all, it can be your reference when thinking about the tasks. You might want to track the usage of your current resources so the documentation can become handy. You might also want to see the assessment process for future reference when needing to make the same kind of decision. The chance to look at the process again can be put into good use for the future. When you need to remember it again for various purposes, you can just look at the notes that you have made.

The allocation of limited resources for your to-do list also has to sometimes pay attention to other people's use as well. There might be some people who you use the resources together with. For a simple illustration, the resource of the meeting room facility in your office might be shared with other people. You cannot simply use the resource for your purpose without concerning the others. For that, take a look at your assessment result. If the task with the shared resource should be done, then you need to communicate it with other people immediately. Thus, other people will not book the utilization of the resource prior to your task implementation. They can also allocate their time to do some other activities unrelated to the use of the resources. That situation should give productivity advantages to you and them.

# ACHIEVABLE APPROACH #3: CONSIDER THE MOST EFFECTIVE WAYS

One benefit by having a limitation is you can force yourself to think about the best utilization of the limitation. By having no other choices, it can trigger your creative thinking to open the path for great actions ideas. Those great actions may give you the best outcomes that won't be considered if you don't have the limitation. Another advantage is the limitation can be used for the task implementation in other manners which might be more beneficial.

This situation can be also true regarding the limitation that you have when you formulate your to-do list. Time is one of the greatest concerns when you create your list. The time is limited so you have to think of the ways to utilize it the best way. You cannot put so many tasks to do without considering the limited time that you have. That approach can waste your time as your to-do list becomes too full of tasks that need your time to implement.

This is when the implementation of achievable characteristics in your to-do list can be so important. Regarding this achievable characteristic, one approach is to consider the most effective ways for getting the outcomes that you want. Doing this should enable you to achieve much more with the limited time that you have.

Being able to implement the most effective tasks to get your outcomes can be beneficial in so many ways. Besides getting the outcomes that you want in a faster fashion, you can also do more in less time. You can list more tasks as you formulate your to-do list because they are the effective ways. They should spend less of your time to achieve the outcomes that you want. This is the essence of productivity and that can be gained if you can do the best kinds of tasks. You can also achieve long-term success faster as you move swifter from task to task and complete them.

To implement this achievable approach, think about the shortest ways that can get you from A to B. In the to-do list formulation, the ways are the tasks that you list. The A is your current condition and the B is the outcomes that you want to get. Is there any way you can achieve B by spending a little amount of time? You may need to eliminate the tasks that are not so important to do that. You may also need to combine your tasks so the time spent can be reduced significantly. The concern should be to minimize the effort while maximizing the impact. The more time that can be saved by doing a task, the better.

For example, imagine you have the tasks to work on a presentation for a project result and create report for it. If the contents of them can be made the same, then you might want to do them together. That can significantly save your time to get the outcomes of both tasks. You may also get some insight from each of the tasks that you can use to add value to another. That might result in the best outcomes that you can get from both of the tasks.

If it is possible, you might also want to think about the most effective steps to get your outcomes. When you draw the step-by-step of the task implementation, you might find that some of the steps aren't essential. Eliminate them from your tasks' implementation. You might need to add some notes about the most effective implementation of the tasks. This is to ensure that you do not forget it and can seriously save time when the tasks are being run.

To be effective, you can also concern yourself with the resources that you need to use for the tasks. As you have decided on the tasks that utilize the limited resources in the previous chapter, think about the tasks implementation. You should do the implementation that can be effective with the resources. That means that it can utilize the least resources to produce the optimum outcomes. Think about the implementation of the tasks and ways that you can eliminate resource utilization. Those ways should not affect the quality of the outcomes too much. As you find ways to do that, you might want to take note of them. This can make sure that you remember them during the implementation.

# TIME-BOUND APPROACH #1: SET THE DEADLINE

The time-bound characteristic in a to-do list is about getting clear with the tasks in relation to the time variable. The certainty of when the tasks should be finished will help to ensure that we will get them done in time.

Intending to give this certainty, it is imperative that we set some self-imposed deadlines on our task points. The deadlines will serve as the guide to when we should finish our tasks.

The deadline in a to-do list can be divided into two. They are the deadline to complete each of the tasks and the deadline to complete all tasks in the to-do list. The deadline of the whole to-do list, of course, depends on the deadline of the tasks in it. Therefore, when you want to set the deadline for each task, think about the time you need to complete all tasks. This is to ensure that all of them can be completed during the period of your to-do list. As you have done the exercise to make the list achievable in terms of time, that practice should help you. The results of that previous assessment can be used to set the deadline to your tasks.

Now, remember: what is the minimum time that you need to spend for each of the tasks? Set the deadline for the tasks by writing the time down as a note in your to-do list. Write the time in your day when you should finish your tasks based on the time. That should help to remind you with the time-bound aspect of your tasks. The note can become the guide that you use to help to ensure that the tasks are done on time. The deadlines are set. Now, it is up to you to complete the tasks in your to-do list within the time frame given.

If what you work on is not a daily to-do list, then you might need to set the date deadline too for your list. Write the dates when you can finish all of your tasks as fast as possible. You might need to prioritize the tasks as the most important ones should be worked first. Setting them should also help you to plan your days so you can finish them early.

When you have deadlines from other people for your tasks, it will benefit you if you impose stricter self-deadlines. For example, if the tasks are due 2 weeks from now, then you should set faster deadline for yourself. Probably 1 week or even few days from now if it is possible. That way, you should have less external pressure when you try to finish it and can work more optimally. If you commit to it, the self-imposed deadline should also give you a chance to check again your work results. The checking can be done by yourself or by other people whose opinion you think is valuable. This most likely boost the quality of your work results. You can be surer with the outcomes of that work as a result.

When setting deadline of your to-do list tasks, you may need to look at the next to-do lists you will formulate. Some of the tasks that you think about are important but might be needed to be finished next time. Therefore, you might need to remember them so you can list the tasks later. To help you do that, you can make a note regarding those future tasks. When you create later to-do lists, you can check the notes again so you can remember about them.

Regarding future tasks, try to also add the date deadlines when you expect them to be completed while you note them. That should help to put the tasks in the right to-do list in the future. Just remember, though, that the condition can change from the current one. The tasks may not be appropriate to be finished again at the set dates because of the condition change. For example, there might be some tasks come up in the future or the noted tasks become redundant. Thus, the date deadlines in the note should just serve as a guide which does not have to be adhered firmly. You may not need to do the tasks again given the circumstances in the future.

Regarding the current to-do list, you might also want to consider to be harder to yourself regarding deadlines. After all, it can determine the productivity that you have from your to-do list especially regarding the time utilization. Think about the optimal time when you can finish each of the tasks and impose them. Commit yourself to finish the tasks according to those strict deadlines so you can realize the highest productivity. The time that you have, after all, is limited and precious. Try to optimize the space on your to-do list so you can do tasks as many as possible. To do that, you need to set the deadlines which can accommodate those tasks. As long as they make sense based on your thinking, then you should try to impose them for yourself.

# TIME-BOUND APPROACH #2: ALLOCATE SPECIFIC TIME IN THE SCHEDULE

The next time-bound approach for our to-do list tool is related to the schedule we have. When trying to estimate the time value for our tasks, you cannot neglect its strong relation to your timetable. A specific time in the schedule can probably change the task that we should do in that period. It will be great if we can connect our tasks with the schedule that we have in the day. We can be more aware of the implication that a certain period will have on the tasks we have in hand.

For illustration, there is certainly the implication of the period in a day to our meeting tasks. After all, the adversaries in the meeting will not have all day to meet as they have other works scheduled. There might be also a certain time that we can finish the report tasks in our to-do list, for example. This is because during the process of the report formulation, we might need to discuss it with our colleagues. They might not be available in some period of the day. Therefore, to be surer with the tasks that we have in our list, we need to check our daily schedule periods. We may able or not be able to put the tasks according to them.

Allocating our tasks in the periods of our schedule should also make us surer with the deadline we have. As we know the period when we work our tasks, we will know better when we should finish them. That will make the tasks more organized and can support the productivity in each period. By being more certain with our tasks schedule periods, we can ensure that we will be readier to work on them. The to-do list will be easier to be implemented and as a result, our productivity should be improved too.

So, what can we do to link the tasks in our to-do list with the specific time in our schedule? Well, this should be simple.

You have learned to set up the deadline in your to-do list from the previous chapter. Now, you look at your schedule in the day to be surer about the period when you will do the tasks. Add the note about the period when you will do the tasks on the to-do list. When doing this, you might discover that some tasks are not compatible to be put in together according to the schedule. It might be because they should occupy the same period of the day. There might also be some tasks that should not be allocated in your to-do list looking at the periods available. Considering the specific time in your schedule when formulating a to-do list can bring important perspectives that affect the tasks.

By utilizing schedule, you can also improve your productivity by allocating the right tasks in their best period. For example, you might be better to create a presentation after lunch because of your supervisor's presence. You can ask his perspective about what you need to add in it while you create it. In the other time of your schedule, he might be busy with other things. Adding the perspective of schedule might help you produce better outcomes. There are some opportunities you might not be able to access at other periods of the day.

By knowing the allocated periods of your tasks in the to-do list, you should be more disciplined. You have known some benefits that you can get from the periods for your tasks during the list formulation. So, you should be more motivated to stick to your to-do list. Having your tasks in periods should also serve as the improvement to your commitment to them. You might need to alter a bit of the schedule as you run through your day. However, you should keep the management of the tasks as tight as possible. This mindset can also help to complete your to-do list by being helped from the scheduling firmness.

You should also take advantage of the schedule by allocating the tasks which are more important first. If there are no special requirements for the period of other tasks, you should do this. It can ensure that they are finished in your day. If you put them at the back, then they may have to wait a turn before other tasks are finished. Work the tasks that you think are the most important ones first. That way, you make sure your to-do list can at least getting them marked as done in your day. It will be important in the event you cannot complete all the tasks in your to-do list.

# TIME-BOUND APPROACH #3: SEE THE LONG-TERM

As has already been described previously, the works that you do will have short-term and long-term results. The short-term results are probably obvious and can be seen not long after you finish the tasks. The long-term ones are not so obvious and you should direct your focus to it if you want to achieve them. After all, it can be that you work just for the short-term results without paying attention to the long-term. This is when you work for what it can directly give you without considering the long-term implications.

When you want to add time-bound characteristics to your to-do list, it can be beneficial to see the long-term results. What are the results that you want to achieve and when do you want to do that? If you know when you want your long-term results, then it can boost the productivity of your works. After all, as with the set deadlines approach, you know when you should get these results from your work. The long-term results are usually achieved by accumulating your work results. If you cannot work as soon as possible, then it is hard to achieve the deadline set for your long-term results. That is because if you are late in your current work, then you will start late for the next tasks. The low productivity will accumulate to make it longer for you to get the long-term results. That should be avoided if you want to commit to the time constraint that you have set.

And that is when your to-do list implementation will get improved also. You will be more encouraged to put more tasks for the long-term results. This is because you want to get them as soon as possible so you can meet your deadlines. Your to-do list will become more of a guide that can help to boost your productivity. It is filled with the tasks that you need to finish fast so you can get the long-term results.

What you should do to optimize the long-term focus for your productivity benefits? Well, first, you have to set the long-term results that you want to get in general from your work. Then, you need to set motivating deadlines for your long-term results. Think about the ideal time when you should achieve them. From there, set the time-bound characteristic to your to-do lists according to your long-term results deadline. It should help you to be more motivated to put in the tasks to make you productive from the to-do list.

Think about the details of your to-do list and those long-term results that you have set. Will these details you have formulated bring you to meet the long-term results and their deadlines? Your target should be working with high productivity so you can do that. Create your to-do list with the mindset to get the long-term results and realize its time-bound element. Make it so you can get there with the guide of your list. You should have more desire to accomplish more tasks by using this time-bound approach for the long-term results.

The time-bound approach in the long-term can also be related to the general situation in life. If you want it to be changed for the better, then you simply have to work your tasks. Not working means that you depend on other people for the change. When you think about it, there is no person more concerned about you than yourself. It is very unlikely that other people will want to work hard for your favor. So, you might as well work hard on your own to change your situation.

If you want the change of the situation to happen fast, then you need to do your work fast too. That can be helped by the right formulation of your to-do list. Add it to your mind when you make the to-do list that you can change the situation faster with your effort. You should let the formulation of the to-do list to reflect this thought. Add the tasks that can make it faster for you to develop the situation around you positively. As you are guided with the to-do list, you should be able to do your best effort with high productivity. That is if you are committed to complete the tasks in your to-do list.

The time-bound characteristic for the long-term results is as important as when it is applied to your tasks and short-term results. If you are focused on getting both results, you should be able to get the best outcomes from your tasks. It can be helped by your to-do list formulation. The to-do list that has concern for both can support you to get results by improving your tasks' focused productivity.

# SUCCESS-ORIENTED APPROACH #1: HAVE YOUR GRAND GOAL IN MIND

Want to succeed in life? Your to-do list can be the tool that you need to realize that for you. Success is the accumulation of the effort that is directed towards it, after all. If you want to achieve success with your to-do list, then you need to have success-oriented characteristics in it. To do that, one of the approaches that can be done is to always have that success in your mind. Especially the time when you formulate your to-do list.

Having the grand goal in mind, which is your success, can help your effort to realize it. When you formulate your to-do list, think whether the tasks in it are relevant to that goal. If it is, then the task can be great to have on your to-do list. If it is not and your to-do list is dominated by it, then evaluate the content of your to-do list. Are you seriously want to achieve your success? If you do, then there is no reason to do too many tasks that are not related to it. The more time you spend working on something else, the more time you cannot utilize to progress to your success achievement.

As you have read few times in the previous chapters, time is a limited resource for us all. The way you do things at a time will eliminate your chance to do other things at the same time. Therefore, you should allocate your working hours as much as possible for tasks related to your success.

If it is possible, then it will be better if you can allocate your to-do list for the relevant tasks only. That should help you achieve success faster. Imagine if you can use all your working hours to do just the things that are in line with your success. Your progress should be great and fast. It can add itself up gradually.

This situation means that you have consistently worked hard towards your success. That is the main prerequisite to achieving what you want in life as it seems.

If you want to have a grand goal in mind during to-do list formulation, however, you should first define it. What is the success that you want in life from your work? The answer can be many things and it can be different for each person. You may like to be rich, have a harmonious family, have a great social impact, or other things. Most of the time, you may even have more than one success that you want to achieve. It is important, though, that you can keep the focus on the success that you want. Having too many targets can distract you and make your to-do list unfocused. The maximum of 5, like what Warren Buffet suggests in his famous 5/25 rule, should be good. That way, you can do the tasks which are not too diverse in terms of their purpose.

From there, you can set your to-do list according to the success definition of yours. When you formulate your to-do list, think about the achievement of those targets. What can you do to get yourself closer to that achievement? Write the tasks that can associate themselves with those targets.

If you don't have a clear success definition, then it is surely hard to formulate your to-do list based on it. That is just logical. After all, what is the thing that you want to base on? Having a fuzzy definition of your success can be one of the reasons why is it so hard to achieve it. Therefore, make the definition formulation as one of the priority tasks that you should do. That is if you want your to-do list to have success-oriented characteristics.

When you need to refer to your success definition often, it can help if you document it somewhere. This is so just you can easily look at it every time you need it. Just take it out when you try to formulate your to-do list. Take a look at the documentation every time you start your to-do list formulation. If you formulate your to-do list regularly, then the habit may leave a strong memory of the success on your mind. You will remember your success definition easily as you go through the day. That should help you too in directing your activities towards it.

As with the short-term and long-term results of your tasks, it will help if you can allocate the deadline. It will bring more commitment to you for working to realize it. If you document your success, then write it with the deadline attached to it. It should remind you every time you make your to-do list so you are more motivated for your tasks. That can boost your productivity to realize your success as soon as possible.

# SUCCESS-ORIENTED APPROACH #2: PRIORITIZE THE MOST IMPORTANT ONES

In the tasks that you have formulated in your to-do list, there are some which are more important. The important criteria can be different between one person and another. Thus, the prioritization process of the tasks can be different too. However, if you want to be success-oriented, then it is better to have criteria according to the success definition. That can surely help you in getting closer to your success from your effort every day.

When you do it, you should ask yourself this question: how will this task help me to achieve success? The ones that you should prioritize to do simply are the ones which can help you the most. If you can do the prioritization process excellently, then your time utilization can be impactful. You should be able to progress yourself to success fast. The prioritization should boost your productivity related to your success achievement.

Doing the prioritization of your tasks during the to-do list formulation can bring many benefits. Besides getting the most influential outcomes to your success quicker, you can also throw away the most unimportant tasks. They are the tasks that will have no to little impact on your success. As you try to prioritize the important ones, they should be kept away in your to-do list. Another benefit is to get yourself the habit of doing important tasks only. As you keep on organizing your tasks according to their importance, your working mindset can be improved. Gradually, you should be smarter in selecting the work that is related and unrelated to your success. The lessons from the experience can be invaluable for your success achievement. You can learn to say no to unmeaningful kinds of tasks during the process.

To start prioritizing, to be thorough, you may want to assess each of the tasks to help you do it. Do the assessment based on how easy the task can be done and how big is the impact on success progress. Add more weight for the impact if you think that helps. Gives the score for each of the variables before you add the scores. This should give you the final scores for the basis of their prioritization. Assess for each of the tasks which you think are potential to be included in your to-do list. If you don't have the time, then you might want to just do a quick mental exercise on this.

You should get some results related to the assessment process. From the result, you should be able to do the prioritization process easily based on quantitative factors. The ones with the highest scores should be prioritized. You can also set some minimum requirements for the tasks to enter your to-do list. If the score is below your minimum requirement, then they can be discarded and not worked at all. Be smart when you do this, though, so you don't miss anything important you should do. You do not want to cross something that is needed to be done even if they don't look impactful.

If you need it, then you can also discuss with relevant people to the success related to the prioritization. When it is related to your work, then you may want to discuss it with your colleague or supervisor. If it is related to family matters, then you can get valuable feedback from your spouse or other family members. Discuss with them what do they think the prioritization should be. After that, think on your own to decide which task should be prioritized. Their feedbacks might become important inputs for the process.

You should, of course, consider the external deadlines that you have too regarding the tasks. The deadlines that are imposed by other relevant people cannot be ignored. Especially when those people are a crucial part of your success. You may need to prioritize the tasks with tight deadlines from them. If this is the case, then you should include the external deadlines to your prioritization factor. Consider the time when you should turn in the works. As has been mentioned in the deadline chapter, it will be better if you can finish them faster. That will give you a breathing room and should result in better outcomes.

Tasks prioritization process in your to-do list formulation can boost your productivity-related to success. When your success is the prime criteria for the approach, you should be able to work only on the impactful tasks. Consider the deadline, the ease of implementation, and the impact that they can give. By juggling them in the best way, the to-do list should significantly help in bringing progress to your success achievement.

# SUCCESS-ORIENTED APPROACH #3: REFLECT ON THE PROGRESS

Your success, especially if the gap you try to bridge is large, may need a long time to work on time. In that period, you need to keep putting in the effort and improve yourself based on your experience. Those things that you do, of course, should be relevant to the success that you want to chase. The direction of your works needs to be kept in the same way towards your success.

If you want to keep doing your effort while improving along the way, you should do a regular evaluation process. This is related to the success-oriented approach, which is doing reflection of your success progress. When you utilize a to-do list tool, you should evaluate your implementation constantly. You need to ask yourself: what are the things you have done for the task listing and how are the completion? You may find something that you can use to improve your to-do list significantly as you think about it.

The reflection on the progress must be done from time to time as you implement the to-do list. When you reflect, it should be the moment when you think how can you do better. Maybe the to-do list implementation has not bought the productivity benefit that you want. Probably your to-do list can be improved in terms of the organization to your work. It might still not list the tasks that you think are crucial for your success. After the reflection is done, you should have the ideas to implement your to-do list in the best way. Thus, the tool can guide you to progress better to the success that you want.

In the case of your success achievement, you should direct the reflection process to your success progress. Think about the way your to-do list can serve you better in terms of your success achievement. In general, the productivity benefit that you get from the to-do list should correlate directly with the success progress. After all, the more productive you are, the faster you should achieve success. The more you do in less time, the accumulation of your effort for success should be done quicker too.

However, you should be careful of this kind of reflection perspective. The productively done tasks should be all directed to your success achievement if you want to succeed. Even if you are productive in doing your tasks, they can be not relevant to the success that you want. In that case, it should be considered as not good and you should fix the future implementation. You should include more tasks that can support your success progress. If most of the tasks in your to-do list do not support your success, then they are done with little meaning.

The reflection on the progress is done so you can move faster to your success. Thus, to get the optimum benefit, you should do the activity regularly. This is so you can keep on improving yourself along the way. The reflection process can be done daily as you make your daily to-do list and in another longer period. In this period, you should allocate a special time to think about the reflection. This is done to make you able to evaluate your implementation in the previous period and the improvement you should do. The scale of the evaluation is much bigger so that is why you might need to allocate special time for this.

This period of evaluation besides daily can be like monthly, three months, or any other period. During this evaluation process, you should do a bigger evaluation process for your to-do list implementation. It should be related to the success progress. For example, if you choose to do it monthly, then think about your to-do list implementation in the previous month. Did it already help you in the best way to be productive for your success progress? Then think about the things that you can do to be better in the next month. This big period evaluation process may capture the things that you don't capture in the daily evaluation. It is because the picture that you see should be much broader than the daily ones.

To do the reflection on your success progress better related to your to-do list, allocate enough time for it. If it is the daily evaluation process, then probably 15-30 minutes should do as you formulate your next to-do list also. If it is the other period evaluation, then it might need more time. When you do this kind of evaluation process, allocate this evaluation task also in your to-do list. Thus, you won't forget to do it as it can be important to optimize the benefits you get from the tool. Especially the ones related to the productivity of your success achievement.

# ACCESSIBLE APPROACH #1: WRITE IT SOMEWHERE

When you try to implement the accessible characteristic to your to-do list, then, first, you should simply make the list visible. You may think that it is already enough to have the task list in your mind. However, it is often the case of forgetting the tasks that you have thought about previously. Therefore, documentation of your to-do list is important during the list formulation. To do the documentation, you have to write the list of tasks somewhere that you can refer to later. This should make your to-do list easier to be accessed rather than just trusting your mind to remember it for you.

Writing the tasks that you add to your to-do list can have some advantages for you. The obvious one is the to-do list can become a reference that you can look into anytime you need it. You can also help the reflection process of your to-do list formulation to make its implementation much better in the future.

As has been told in the previous chapter, you should look at the productivity benefits you get from your list. By having a note of the tasks that you should complete previously, it can be easier in evaluating your productivity. You should improve the way you formulate your to-do list easier as a result.

By having your to-do list written, you will also not forget the tasks undone at the end of the day. Going through the day, you might forget the details of your work as your mind keeps shifting focus on different things. Getting the documentation of what you should do can also make you easier to continue the tasks if they aren't completed. It can be an important reference for the next day's to-do list. Especially if the tasks are something you should do fast.

Is there anything you should pay attention to when you try to write your to-do list? First of all, it can be better if you write it using the traditional way instead of typing it. Research says that writing by hand allows your brain to focus more on the things that you write. As a result, you should be able to remember more about your tasks when you write your to-do list that way. This can be a benefit if you don't want to keep looking on your to-do list. Writing by hand can also be a cognitive exercise that your brain needs. As you usually formulate your to-do list daily, the writing process can be a regular workout for your mind. It should help your mind to keep being sharp and maintain your brain function as a result.

When you write your tasks, you should also pay attention to the medium where you write it. If possible, then you should write it in the place where you can keep the past to-do list documentation in one. Mediums such as a notebook or journal should be good in keeping the documentation of your to-do list. This is related to the evaluation process that you might want to do with your to-do list later.

Moreover, you may also want to keep tab on the tasks that have not been completed, as has been told earlier. By having your writing where you can keep history, you should be able to do those things easier. You can easily look at the past to-do lists and see what are the tasks being done from them. As a result, you can measure your productivity in the past and learn how you can improve it. You can also know the tasks that you must complete later as a continuation of the things you have done previously.

If you have long-term results and success definition as suggested before, then it is good if you can write them here. This is done so you can easily take a look at them during the formulation of your to-do list. After all, it is easy to forget about those long-term things during your to-do lists formulation when you cannot see them. By writing them in the same medium, you should be able to focus your tasks more to those desired future results. Have them written somewhere in the medium along with the important notes such as deadlines. That should help you keep yourself on your toes regarding the tasks that you have to list. The most important thing is, of course, that you will progress yourself faster to your defined ideal condition in the future. This writing process can be an additional tool for you to keep remembering the long-term goals of your work.

# ACCESSIBLE APPROACH #2: MAKE IT EASY TO KEEP CLOSE

As you have your to-do list written somewhere, another important thing is to make that writing is close by to you. The to-do list that you have formulated should act as your guide to do important works during your day. Therefore, getting it somewhere that you can take a look easily when you need it should be prioritized. By having your to-do list close by, you shouldn't forget the things that you have to work on during the day. After all, it is just a glance away from where you are when you go through your daily activities.

Having your list somewhere you can access easily should help in disciplining yourself with the tasks that you should do. There should be no reason that you forget those tasks when you can easily take a look at them. By making your list easily accessible anytime, therefore, there should be more commitment to finish what you have to work on. It should also give more chance to have you complete the to-do list that you have formulated. The ability to take a look at your list anytime can ensure that you keep building momentum to finish your tasks. After you finish one task, you can take a look to see what is the next thing that you should do. One thing after another, it should help you increase your productivity in finishing the to-do list that you have formulated. Your to-do list has a higher chance to be completed as a result.

Principally, to make your to-do list close by, it should be easy. If you have your list written in a notebook or journal as suggested earlier, then you should keep that medium close. Probably, you can put it on your desk or have it ready in your bag that you put near your work station. If you find these ways inconvenient, then you can also take a picture on the to-do list from your smartphone. Or maybe it will be easier for you if you write them down in a to-do list app which you can access anytime. There, you can easily take a look at the to-do list from your gadget which you usually keep close by. By utilizing the media available to keep your to-do list somewhere close, you should have no trouble in making it accessible.

To ensure the to-do list writing is close by, you should have a habit of bringing along your to-do list. Especially during the time and place which you usually work. Wherever you put your to-do list, put it in your bag or other things you usually bring to your work. Only take it out when you should create your to-do list or reflect on your productivity benefits from the tool. This should ensure that you don't forget to bring your to-do list as you go through the day. You may also want to do a habit of making sure that it has been brought before you run your activities. Check the stuff that you bring again as you prepare yourself to begin the day. This should make sure that your to-do list will stay accessible when you need it anytime.

Making your to-do list accessible by keeping it close should also be helped by trying to be not forgetful about it. Besides checking things you bring before you do activities, you can also place it on the internet if you have to. Doing that will ensure that it can be seen anytime anywhere by you and you will not forget it. If you choose this way, then you should make it a habit to upload your to-do list after you formulate it. Using the internet media should also ensure that you can have a place to save the history of your to-do lists. You can easily take a look at them anytime anywhere that you want to.

There are obviously some ways you can keep your to-do list close by, as you can see in the explanation above. You should choose the one which you think is most convenient for you. You should also choose the way which can guarantee the most that you can keep your to-do list close by. By having the discipline of doing that, you should improve the chance to be productive from your to-do list. Your day can be run as you plan it when you formulate your to-do list to organize your most important works.

# ACCESSIBLE APPROACH #3: PLACE REMINDERS

As you go through your day, you can be prone not paying attention to the to-do list that you have formulated. This can happen even if you have implemented the previous accessible approaches which are: write the list and keep it close. As you have many things to do, it can be easy to forget the list close by to you.

The limited capacity to remember important works can be dangerous to the right kind of productivity that you want to have. Productivity should be focused on the tasks which are important and meaningful for you. After all, that is one of the main purposes why you formulate your to-do list, right? It is so you complete the important tasks that you have during your day. You want to finish the task points which are listed in your to-do list.

These important tasks that you must do should be your to-do list function as it helps you to remember them. But you can still easily miss it as you focus too much on the task at hand. You may neglect to take a look at the tasks you have listed even when it is crucial that you do so.

If you run into this problem, then you should do something to prevent it to happen. For that, this accessible approach for your to-do list should help you to do it. The approach suggested is to place reminders for tasks that you have listed in your to-do list. They are there to particularly remind you of the most important tasks on the list.

Placing reminders for your to-do list can be important and a key factor to complete the list you have formulated. Besides helping you to remember to do the tasks in it, this accessible approach can also help to improve your productivity. As you place your reminders, there can be a greater memory about the time limit you have to finish a task. This factor can drive you more to finish your task within the ideal time given by your to-do list. Moreover, having reminders can also make you more aware of the relative importance of your task completion. You can find that you have a reminder to move to the next task while you haven't finished the previous task. At that time, you can choose which task is more important and what to do with the task you delay. Without reminders, you might be much more inclined in continuing the current task until it is finished. There are some moments when it is better to do the next task first rather than continuing your current task. Having something to remind yourself at the next task can be the trigger for you to get into the consideration process.

So, let us see how best we should implement this approach for the accessible characteristic of your to-do list. First, when you want to place reminders in your to-do list, then you must skim through the tasks you have listed. There might be tasks that don't have to be completed at that time or day. Some tasks, however, are simply must be or should be done in the period that is attributed to them. See the nature of your tasks according to this group division. Obviously, you should place reminders on tasks that should be completed in the time or day you have given for them. Try to do the reminders placement at the end of the task listing process of your to-do list. At that time, it should be clearer what are the tasks you have and how you should treat each of them.

In the case of the reminders, then you should consider the tools that can be used according to your situation. There are tools such as calendar apps or software which you can use to give yourself a reminder for your tasks. They can be run online or offline according to your preference. These calendar apps or software should be equipped with notification settings that can turn on for things you add in it. By setting them, when you take a look at your gadget or laptop occasionally, you can see the notification. You should set the notification to be activated when the time is near for you to do the task. Remember to note correctly the given day and time for the tasks in the tool that you use for reminders.

You can also use reminders such as alarms if you think that it can help you better in remembering your tasks. They can be set in your gadget and the sound that it makes should help you greatly in remembering important tasks. Just be sure to use the reminder tools that are appropriate and the most effective for your situation. The right reminder tools should help you in your effort to complete all the tasks in your to-do list.

# FINAL WORDS: COMMITMENT ON THE IMPLEMENTATION

The approaches introduced in this book may take some time to implement. This often happens, particularly when you have just done them for the first few times. As you get used to creating your to-do list in the suggested way, it should be gradually easier for you. Before long, you will know what you miss if you haven't implemented part of the approaches. You should also begin to get the improved productivity benefits that you need from your to-do list by that time. That should be the case as you have implemented the right approaches in the tool implementation consistently.

When you decide you want to use a to-do list to organize your works, you must expect some benefits from it. It is not wrong as the tool should be popular for a reason. The list has long been something that is used to improve productivity by many people. They have felt the advantages that can be had by using it and so are you too. However, it is important that we know how to implement it correctly to guide our activities through the days. As has been explained previously, the wrong implementation can nullify the benefits or even becomes a new source of unproductivity. This is what we try to avoid as we discuss the approaches you can use to make an excellent to-do list. After all, we all implement a to-do list to make our works productive, not the opposite.

Productivity is something important for all of us who do work. By having a high level of it, you can ensure that you are able to do more in less time. In terms of doing more, you should also be certain that the things done are the ones that matter. This should ensure that the time that you spend on them is not utilized on the unimpactful things for you.

Formulating a to-do list regularly can help you greatly in making sure that you do the right work. It can also support the effectiveness and efficiency of the time utilization that you spend on those works. However, to get that effect, you should ensure the to-do list contains important works and have the right attributes in it. That is the way in which this tool can give a significant contribution to the improvement of your productivity.

This can be more of the case if you have a definition of success that you want to achieve in life. If you target long-term success, then the to-do list that works for you can provide the guide to achieve it. Most successful people know success is a result of the accumulation of the effort that we do most of the time. Having a to-do list that helps organizing your work can support you focus your effort on the success that you want. It may take some time to achieve your success as it is something that most likely won't be produced instantly. However, as you keep directing the tasks that you list towards it, sooner or later you should make it. Getting the productivity benefits associated with the right to-do list won't hurt. After all, the faster you work, the faster it should be for the success to arrive in your life.

Helping you to create a to-do list that can help to improve your productivity and achieve success is important. That is one of the main reasons why I write this book. Having much experience in the to-do list formulation myself, I keep on trying to improve my implementation of the tool. Learning what other people thought about formulating an optimal to-do list helps me in doing that improvement. The results of the to-do list implementation experience and the learnings are what is provided as the content of this book. I hope they can provide you what you need in terms of creating a to-do list that gives you optimum benefits. In helping you do that,

I hope to support you to achieve productivity and accomplish the success you desire.

In this book, we have talked so much about the to-do list as a tool that helps to organize your tasks. We have discussed how the wrong to-do list can impact negatively on productivity in the early part of the book. To help you avoid creating this kind of to-do list, the next part discussed the seven mistakes of the to-do list. They are the wrong things to do during its formulation and implementation. They can make the tool less beneficial to support you in accomplishing your tasks. We discussed each of the seven mistakes in deep so you can avoid those mistakes as you utilize this tool.

After we discussed those to-do list mistakes, we have also talked about the suggested to-do list characteristics to mitigate them. There are seven characteristics of an excellent to-do list to answer each of the seven mistakes directly. In this part of the book, we talked about them in-depth too. Particularly why they are important and how they can help you to prevent committing the to-do list mistakes. These seven characteristics are: exact, measurable, ambitious, achievable, time-bound, success-oriented, and accessible. You can abbreviate the characteristics to **EMAATSA** to help you remember them in your to-do list implementation. Having them in your to-do list should be a hint that your list can help you to become highly productive.

However, after we know the characteristics of a great to-do list, what are the ways to have them in our list? This is discussed at length at the part which you should have already read too. After the discussion of the characteristics, we discuss the approaches of implementing the seven to-do list characteristics. Each characteristic is given three approaches that you can use to make sure that your to-do list has the characteristic. Each of the approaches has also been given its own part in the book so you know better about them. The approach explanation is mostly about the why and the how parts of it. It is so you have no doubt to implement it straight away in your to-do list after reading the book.

After reading this book, you should have the insight that you need to implement the to-do list that works for you. The kind of list that gives you optimum benefits related to improving productivity and accelerating your success achievement.

So, what's next after you already have this knowledge?

Obviously, what comes after that is the application of what you have known. This might be the most important step for your to-do list implementation. After all, you won't receive any benefits to your list if you just let the knowledge sit in your mind. Without any action that you do, the knowledge gained from this book is in vain.

Therefore, try to immediately implement it in your situation and see it for yourself the approaches suitability. The approaches description written here are not written in stone and should be implemented accordingly. Maybe the approaches suggested in this book need some little tweaks here and there to optimize their implementation for you. Maybe you will find extra details that can work more for you after you have tried to do the implementation. However, you will know those things only when you have tried the approaches. You will have zero knowledge about the detail of the implementation that works for you otherwise.

So, try to build the positive habit of implementing the to-do list that works starting now. Use the knowledge that you have got from this book to help you do that. Improve your implementation as you have more experience in applying the approaches. That should bring you a significant positive impact in terms of productivity and success progress you get from your to-do list.

Are you ready to do this? Let's optimize that to-do list of yours immediately!

# DID YOU LIKE THE TO-DO LIST FORMULA?

First of all, I want to say thanks to you, the reader, for choosing to read this book. It is something that makes me pleased and motivates me to write more books. I hope the content given in here can help you to implement the to-do list that gives you the utmost benefits. Particularly for your productivity improvement and the progress of your success achievement.

With this page too, I want to ask a small favor from you.

If you have a minute or two, then would you mind to give your rating and review for this book? You can do that by going to its amazon page and enter your thoughts about the book there.

As an independent author currently, your thoughts about the content of this book, positive or negative, are very valuable for me. Your feedback, suggestions, and/or inputs will be the thought of consideration for me when I write my next books. I will evaluate them so I can improve myself significantly in my writing.

If you like the book, then please don't hesitate to let me know also ☺.

# MORE BOOKS BY DAN KRISTOPH

\*\*\*\*\*

How to Do What You Love: 3 Phases for Working with Passion and Achieve Success

The Anti-Procrastination Mentality: How to Stop Being Lazy and Get Things Done

Overcoming Failure: How to Turn Failure into Success

Do More Better Faster: The Optimal Outcomes Approach on How to be More Productive and Get More Done in Less Time

Stop Overthinking: How to Relieve Anxiety, Stop Worrying, and Reduce Stress

\*\*\*\*\*

You can see more about the books by visiting his Author Central Page in Amazon:
http://amazon.com/author/dankristoph

# ABOUT THE AUTHOR

The right self-improvement can give you a strong base to achieve what you want in life.

Do you want to be a better person and have a better life? The power of positive habits can help you significantly for that. The condition of your life seems to be created by the habits that you try to implement consistently. The positive habits can propel you to the life that you desire while the bad ones can make you stuck in a bad condition.

Having taken a liking on the subject of self-improvement, drawing the inspiration from the many books that he has read on the topic and the lessons that he has learned through his own life experience, Dan Kristoph tries to share the unique perspective that he has on self-improvement areas in each of his books. Every book that he has written contains comprehensive descriptions and practical suggestions on what are the positive habits that can help you in many aspects of life. Hopefully, by reading some of his books, you can learn and practice the habits that you need to make a better and more positive version of life that you want for yourself.

When he is not writing a book, Dan loves to read self-improvement books (obviously), watch movies, and travel. He loves to joke also though sometimes he is the only one who laughs on it :(

You can visit his blog, Positivity Stories, by visiting the below link:
http://positivitystories.com

www.ingramcontent.com/pod-product-compliance
Lightning Source LLC
Chambersburg PA
CBHW070554220526
45467CB00003B/1210